OPEN D

Copyright © 1994 Derek Baldwin

British Library Cataloguing-in-Publication Data. A catalogue
record for this book is available from the British Library

Published by Highland Books, an imprint of Inter Publishing
Service (IPS) Ltd, 59 Woodbridge Road, Guildford, Surrey
GU1 4RF.

All Scripture quotations, unless otherwise noted, are taken from
The New International Version Copyright © 1973, 1978, 1984 by
the International Bible Society. Used by permission of Hodder &
Stoughton.

Typeset by The Electronic Book Factory Ltd, Fife, Scotland
Printed in the UK by HarperCollins Manufacturing, Glasgow.

ISBN No: 0 946616 87 6

OPEN DOORS
OPEN MINDS

DEREK BALDWIN

HIGHLAND BOOKS
Guildford, Surrey

CONTENTS

FOREWORD

St John's, Boscombe has had an honoured history over the last 100 years as a church with a strong preaching and teaching ministry within the Anglican conservative evangelical tradition. The congregations have included a sizeable proportion of people drawn from a fairly wide area, with the numbers swelled by holiday visitors. The last few years, though, have seen a radical change in its whole style of ministry; from being largely an eclectic, gathered congregation to becoming one that is committed to the locality. In many ways *Open Doors Open Minds* is a remarkable story but it is told by Derek Baldwin without a hint of smugness or triumphalism. It is recounted in a most readable style, with sensitivity, honesty and touches of humour. I was gripped and inspired as each chapter unfolded – especially as what I read matched what I had seen at first hand.

Godfrey Taylor, the Vicar, had shared with his congregation the vision of the church as an Open Door, which would involve far more than simply keeping the church building open. It would mean seeking to be more available to the local community, classified as an urban priority area ranking high in the deprivation scale,

and its many urgent needs. It was a challenge
that the congregation responded to after much
prayer and a thorough survey of the real, rather
than the imagined, composition and needs of the
neighbourhood. It involved the restructuring of
the west end of the church to create a welcoming
centre seven days a week, with many members
of the congregation and other local Christians
being trained and becoming fully involved in the
project.

The translation of a vision into reality requires
not only an enthusiastic response but a shared,
unshakable determination, backed up by prayer,
to see each stage through. The writer pulls no
punches when he describes the set-backs and difficulties that have arisen along the way. Seeking
to respond to such a diverse range of human need
– poor mental health, drug and alcohol addiction,
depressing living conditions, appalling loneliness
– brings enormous demands upon the team of
carers. Learning to listen, and trained to do so,
has become a vital requirement for those involved
in this costly ministry. It is 'feet-washing' of
a highly committed order. But, reflects Derek
Baldwin, 'unless we are as open as our doors
are, this place may still be a place of rejection'.
The greatest single need of those who come is that
of friendship.

Open Doors Open Minds does not, however,
focus solely on one project. It is also about the
setting up in 1985 of a new church centre, now
bursting at the seams, in another part of the
parish, and about the continuing challenge and
encouragement to church members to go out
through the 'Open Door' and share their faith

with others and put it into practical action. There is no room allowed for complacency or marking time, but instead a constant incentive to respond in faith to the call of Jesus Christ to find new and relevant ways of reaching those who are strangers to his transforming love and liberating truth.

The principles and practice of mission embodied and illustrated in this book provide a stimulus and challenge to many other churches in this Decade of Evangelism. It deserves to be widely read.

John Perry
Bishop of Southampton.

PREFACE

Wherever people are referred to in this book using a fictitious name this is made clear in the text. This has been done where it seems pastorally sensitive not to identity them or, in a few cases, where it was not possible or appropriate to ascertain their wishes. All those whose own names are used have given their express permission for this to be done.

I have often had a sneaking feeling that lists of acknowledgements by authors at the start of their books probably owed more to convention than conviction. Finding myself in this position for the first time I now willingly recognise that this is not so.

My sincere thanks, then, to John and Sue Fairbairn, in whose lovely flat overlooking the Isle of Wight most of these pages have been written. I am grateful to a number of people who have read and commented on parts of the manuscript, especially my good friend Harold Wonham, whose perceptive criticism and constant encouragement have more than once been crucial. Also to Betty Lefevre, who coped with my dictation and mastered my word-processor to produce odd bits of draft. And, of course, to my wife Ann, who has had to put up not only with my repeated absences but also with my greater-than-usual absent-mindedness when I was at home.

I should like to thank all those at St John's who have helped with information, support and encouragement, and the whole church family for tolerating my being less active than usual in my 'real' job as their Director of Music during the eight months while this book was being written. It is not for me to say whether or not they have also missed my preaching during that time!

Finally, special thanks are due to Godfrey Taylor, Vicar of St John's. It must be very unusual for a book of this kind about the life of a church fellowship to be written by someone other than its pastor. This cannot have been easy at times, and I should like to record my gratitude both for the freedom he has allowed me and the trust which it represents.

Derek Baldwin
May 1993

Change is the nursery of music, joy, life and
eternity.

John Donne

If anyone is in Christ, he is a new creation;
the old has gone, the new has come!

2 Corinthians 5:17

INTRODUCTION

Some years ago, while taking our children for a day out on the Sussex coast, we found ourselves passing through Newhaven just as one of the car ferries which go from there to Dieppe was preparing to leave. Since I am as fascinated as any child by that kind of thing, we stopped to watch. What we saw has remained in my memory. As it started to move, the ship appeared to be going the wrong way, heading inland up the River Ouse. But once it got away from the quayside it began, imperceptibly at first, to turn round in the harbour. I say 'harbour', but in fact it is really nothing more than the river mouth, not much wider than the length of the ship. Consequently this extraordinary manoeuvre calls for the utmost precision. In the interests of safety it has to be done with great care and takes some time. And a good deal of water is stirred up as the vessel's screws churn away to turn its heavy bulk round and get it moving in the right direction.

That is a fair picture of what this book is about – turning round ... not a ship, but a church. It is always dangerous to press an analogy too far, but there are some striking similarities. Because of the weight and inertia of the body to be turned it

takes some time. The operation certainly stirs up
the water all around, and cannot be accomplished
without creating some sizeable waves. And it must
be done with great care in the interests of safety:
there are passengers on board, every one of them
precious to God.

Let me say at once that when I talk about St
John's, Boscombe turning round, I do not mean
to imply that we were previously going in the
wrong direction and are now going in the right
one. That would not only be arrogant, but it
would also be a quite unwarranted depreciation
of the insights and achievements of previous
generations. It might be nearer the mark to
describe what has been happening in the last
few years as a 'mid-course correction'.

The change to which I am referring is basically
one of outlook. In fact, a great deal of what often
preoccupies us church folk could more accurately
be described as 'inlook'! So much of our time
and energy – and certainly our most animated
discussions – seem to be reserved for strictly 'in'
things such as what service book we use; who may
do what and which way they should face while
they do it; what we wear or refuse to wear, or
the precise minutiae of what we mean by certain
phrases and whether it is compatible with what
others mean by them. All who play any part in
church life will recognise this agenda. Of course,
some of these things are very important – though
it needs to be said that some of them are not! But
they can get quite out of proportion. Then they
become a distraction . . . and meanwhile the world
goes by, taking very little notice of the Church or
the gospel with which we are entrusted.

This attitude of *inlook* is not the prerogative of any particular denomination or 'brand' of churchmanship. Many evangelicals have been brought up to regard their more catholic brothers and sisters as concerned with the externals of religion rather than the preaching of the gospel. Although this might sometimes be true, the evangelical tradition's own tendency towards intense preoccupation with a neatly tied-down package of 'truth' can equally stand in the way of the gospel of the kingdom as Christ taught and demonstrated it. Even the charismatic movement which has brought such a breath of fresh air to the Church can easily fall prey to the same kind of introspection. *Inlook* can affect all kinds of Christians.

Of course these are all gross over-simplifications – some would say to the point of caricature. But then, sadly, we Christians all too frequently settle for stereotyped, often quite inaccurate, images of one another. We all find it easy to look over the fences of our own making and criticise what those on the other side are doing. So you may well fear that this book is going to say 'Look what we're doing . . . just go away and copy it and you'll be on the right track'. Here's another bunch of clever-Dick Christians with a success story to make the rest of us feel like failures. Let me try to put your mind at rest straight away. This book is not a 'success story'. It is not intended to tell anybody where they are going wrong, nor to suggest that we have got it right. Indeed, where there have been mistakes and failures, I hope they are honestly recorded. It is not a DIY manual on church growth, nor a handbook to the Decade of

Evangelism. It simply tells the story of a very
'ordinary' church (not that there can be such a
thing!) and how God is in the process of turning
us round – away from over-preoccupation with
ourselves, our activities and our ways of doing
things, and towards the world and its desperate
needs. Previously St John's existed in a bit of a
vacuum. It is God himself who gave us a new
vision of ourselves in the community, and it is in
working out that vision that we are being changed.
Although some changes have obviously been the
result of conscious decisions by the church and its
leaders, as we look back we are increasingly aware
that it has been God's firm but gentle touch on the
tiller altering our course.

So this book has been written to *encourage* all
who may be feeling the tug of his hand on the
wheel of their lives. This means churches, but also
individuals – one of its main emphases is that in
practice a church can change course only when
enough of its individual members let go and allow
God to steer. And it has been written to *stimulate*
those whose energies are devoted basically to
keeping moving, without much thought for the
direction in which they are going. Lastly I hope it
may *challenge* those whose chief concern is to keep
the vessel afloat, who perceive their task as throw-
ing out the anchor to remain as static as possible
against the changing tides and currents. Their
preoccupation – and it is one they often hold with
great sincerity and pursue with considerable vig-
our – is to keep things as they have always been.
Such people reading this book may well be puzzled
and possibly (though I hope not) irritated by it.

These are stirring times for the Church. There

is a great deal of white water being churned up
. . . particularly around that redoubtable craft the
SS Church of England! As church-planting gathers
pace, the centuries-old parochial system, however
well it may have served the gospel in the past, is
coming under increasing pressure. The women's
ordination has precipitated a crisis which could
have all kinds of consequences: eventually the
Church must face the more fundamental issue of
the nature of ministry. Royal family troubles have,
by a rather tortuous logic, brought the question of
disestablishment higher up the agenda. Renewal
is now used less as a buzzword relating 'to
those who like that sort of thing', and more to
reflect a mature understanding of the Spirit's
contemporary work in churches of all shades
and descriptions. Many are discovering that it
has to do with far more than the charismatic
gifts and distinctive worship style with which
the 'movement' has tended to be identified. I
identify a concept which I believe is coming
into sharper focus in many places as 'renewal
for service'.

That may not sound very revolutionary. In
fact, though, it will probably mean a significant
change of direction – even for churches widely
regarded as 'sound' or 'successful'. It will involve
re-examining old assumptions and changing attitudes and priorities. And changes demand sacrifices. It is exciting, challenging, costly and at times
slightly frightening. A few years ago we could not
have foreseen most of what is happening to us at St
John's. But, now that it is happening, we are very
conscious that it is God's doing. That means that if
it can happen to us, it can certainly happen to you.

CHAPTER ONE

THE CHURCH OF THE OPEN DOOR

"Yer gonna make me, or what?"

He towered above her threateningly, a huge man with a strong Glaswegian accent and an even stronger smell of alcohol hanging around him – not actually drunk, but in that sullen state that shows it is not long since his last drink . . . and not long before he will be wanting another. His manner, as well as his aggressive growl, said plainly that here was a man used to getting his own way; the bruises and scars on his face suggested that in order to get it he would fight all comers when necessary. The person who tried to show him the door was either very brave or very stupid.

In fact she was neither. She was a grey-haired lady – not old, but certainly on the heavenward side of sixty – and while not actually frail, she appeared somewhat fragile. She did not even come up to his shoulder; he could have picked her up and swung her round with one hand. Yet she had just said to him, 'I'm sorry, but if you're going to use that kind of language, I shall have to ask you to leave'. Brave? Not really. She was quaking in her shoes, and she could feel her heart thumping. Stupid? No, not that either. It was simply that she

could not stand by and hear Christ's name used as
this man had just done. Christ was her friend and
her Lord. And so it was almost without thought
for the consequences that she had spoken up, and
with a sudden, strange and unexpected sense of
authority. That Christ's name should blasphemed
here, of all places . . .

Because this was not a pub, and she was not
a barmaid. It was a church; and she was one of
those ladies of a certain age who are to be found
in churches the length and breadth of the land –
the kind who can all too easily be dismissed as
'pew fodder'. What on earth was going on? How
could it be right that such a vulnerable saint was
left in a situation so fraught with danger? It was
not right. It was not what had been planned at
all: but the best laid plans . . . As it happened, the
man went and sat, muttering sulkily, in a corner
for some minutes. Then, when he saw she was
absorbed with another visitor, he slunk quietly
out of the door. He wasn't having her thinking
he left because she had told him to!

Where would he go? He would probably spend
the night huddled under the pier, or in a seafront
shelter. Because this delightful little cameo was
not set in the dingy back streets of a run-down
industrial town, nor in one of the more deprived
districts of London, but in a pleasant South coast
resort. Sun, sand and sea . . . and more hotels
than any other resort in Britain: that may well
be your image of Bournemouth, and it would be
right. But on a bleak, rainy afternoon in February
it can be as miserable and uninviting as anywhere;
and on this particular day the weather had driven
quite a number of people into St John's, Boscombe

seeking warmth, shelter and a free cup of tea.
Many lived in bed and breakfast accommodation,
spending all day looking for somewhere to go
and something to do. Some, like this inebriated
Scotsman, would have nowhere at all to go once
it got to half past four and St John's closed its
doors.

But at least for now they could come in. And
that, in itself, was quite remarkable, because until
recently, like many other town churches, unless
there was a service going on St John's was closed.
Problems of theft and vandalism meant that it
was no longer realistic for the church to be open
without someone in attendance, and you could
hardly expect people to be there all day just in
case one or two bona fide visitors wanted to look
round. There would not be many – St John's has
no medieval stained glass, interesting brasses, or
ornate memorials. There was not even an up-to-
date guide book, and we had not bothered with a
visitors' book for years. The building existed for its
congregation, who used it for perhaps three hours
a week. For the rest of the time there it stood, its
doors closed and locked.

Yet today it is known as the Church of the Open
Door. It stands open every day. Visitors do come in
to look around. But more come in to talk to people
who are friendly and genuinely want to listen and,
where appropriate, offer help and care. Those who
come in may be holidaymakers; they may live in
the area; some are 'on the road' as a way of life,
others just drifting. Whoever they may be, they
are not just *allowed*, but positively *encouraged*, to
come in. Notices on the pavement invite those who
have problems, who are anxious or just lonely, to

come inside and talk. And, as the news has spread,
people come on the recommendation of friends,
or because they have heard through some other
channel of the Church of the Open Door.

* * *

I suppose you might say this all began in the
mid 1980s, when Godfrey Taylor, the present
vicar of St John's, heard from a friend living
in Australia about the remarkable work going
on in the Church of the Open Door in Sydney.
Subsequently David Cohen, who had been Vicar
of that church, visited St John's in his capacity as
the Scripture Union's General Director. He talked
with Godfrey and the germ of an idea was planted.
It would not go away. It grew in the bath. His
ideas usually do. In fact, when regular members
of the congregation hear him say 'in the bath
the other morning, I was thinking . . .', hardly
an eyebrow is raised. Any greater sign of surprise
at the mention of the vicarage bathroom almost
certainly means you are looking at a visitor! But if
people's thoughts appeared in little bubbles above
their head, like in the cartoon strips, you would see
the regulars thinking 'hello . . . now what . . .?'
because experience has taught us that the ideas
emerging from the bath usually mean that sooner
or later – probably sooner – something is going to
change!
  The vision gradually crystallised into a picture
of an open door which involved far more than
simply keeping the church building open. It meant
a new openness to people; a new awareness of the
community in which St John's was set; a new

willingness to engage with the real and urgent
needs of the world around us. The doors were to
be open for people to come in and also for us to go
out. In short, he believed we were being called in
a new way to be open to God, to what he wanted to
show us about being his servants and the agents
of his love in the world.

Of course, we did not see this all at once. But
as Godfrey Taylor reflected and prayed about this
picture which would not go away, and as he began
to share it with others in the church, it slowly
became clear that it might mean all of this and
more. In one sense that is the story told in this
book. And yet, in another sense, it is not: because
it is now apparent that this 'opening up' process
did not begin there, but further back. What is
more, now that the Church of the Open Door has
been a reality for over four years, we can see that
what seemed such a major transformation was
not an end in itself, but only part of a continuing
process.

Where *did* it start? And where will it end? The
first question is difficult to answer, the second
impossible. But both are worth pursuing – not
because our own story is particularly interesting
(though hopefully some readers will be excited
by the dramatic way in which God works in
individuals and a congregation), but precisely
because what is happening at St John's, Boscombe
is *not* unique. In many other Christian communities, large and small, God is awakening his
people to a new commitment to the world around
them. With this comes a greater sense of urgency
about the need to reach out to those who, in
our increasingly secularised society, have had no

contact whatsoever with the Christian message.
It is with such people that we are called to share
the gospel of Jesus Christ. Writing in the *Church
Times* in September 1992, Michael Green said that
amongst the elements which would be involved
for any church which was going to make real
advances in evangelism, would be the development
of every-member ministry, involvement with the
local community 'in its joys, struggles and needs'
and 'welcoming, joyful services, full of praise and
prayer, teaching and silence'.

For some churches, this agenda would be slightly
unreal, if not completely alien. Others might find
it intimidating. I suspect that for most it would
represent, if not a complete U-turn, at least a
significant change of direction. For us at St John's
it would have seemed a tall order a few years ago.
Yet, amazingly, it could almost have been written
as a description of our recent experiences . . . if not
as a list of achievements, at least as a statement
of aims. I believe this is a significant aspect of
the Holy Spirit's renewal of the Church in this
final decade of the century. If so, it is important
that we learn from one another's experiences. The
story of what God is doing for us and through us
at St John's may be used to encourage, challenge,
stimulate or guide others who are themselves at
a point where they may either grow or dwindle –
either become more effective as God's witnesses
to an unbelieving society, or give up altogether.

CHAPTER TWO
THE CHURCH AT THE CROSSROADS

Boscombe is just one part of the conurbation which sprawls along some eight miles of coastline in central southern England. Christchurch to the east with its Norman priory, and Poole to the west, once one of England's principal ports, both have their roots deep in the region's history. In between lies Bournemouth, a relatively recent upstart, owing its existence almost entirely to the nineteenth-century fad for 'the seaside'. As the town expanded rapidly with the arrival of the railway, Boscombe became one of the premier fashionable areas.

In 1895, when St John's Church was built, it was a pleasant 1/4-mile walk through the woods to the sea. You would never guess that today as it stands at a busy crossroads, surrounded by buildings and the noise of traffic pulling away from the lights. Designed by John Oldrid Scott in fourteenth-century 'Middle Decorated' style, it seated almost 1,200 people. The exterior, devoid of tower or spire and faced with dark knapped flints, is unprepossessing. Step inside and you are surprised by a lofty interior of pale, gleaming Bath stone, beautiful and impressive.

The second half of the nineteenth-century saw
an explosion of urban church building across
England. But St John's was built not just for a
growing population, but for a very specific purpose – to meet a deeply-felt need for an Anglican
ministry of evangelical character in the district.
That purpose has shaped its first hundred years
with remarkable consistency. To understand the
full significance of this it is necessary to do a little
church history.

Nineteenth-Century Origins

It is difficult for us to imagine the world in which
our Victorian forbears lived and worshipped. In
Great Britain today the general climate is one of
mutual toleration, if not respect, between Christians of different denominations and traditions;
while those outside the churches are generally
ignorant of the issues which might divide Christians. Things were very different throughout the
nineteenth-century: an informed animosity existed
between Protestants and Roman Catholicism. Par-
liament dealt with a flood of contentious religious
issues, progressively removing the obstacles in
education and public life which had disadvantaged Roman Catholics in England and Wales
since the Reformation. This new freedom was
matched by growing numbers of people convert-
ing to Roman Catholicism, which caused deep
concern amongst Protestant Christians, especially
amongst evangelicals. At times that concern reached
fever pitch, spilling over into acrimonious charges
and counter-charges. These were widely taken up,

even by the man in the street: today's distinction
between a churchgoing minority and the largely
unconcerned masses outside simply did not exist.
Many could still remember anti-Popery street
riots, and the issues had national rather than
purely ecclesiastical significance.[1]

Developments within the Anglican Church exacerbated matters. In the 1830s and 40s the Oxford
Movement enthusiastically reminded English
Christians of their catholic roots. Its founders
had a deep spirituality and zeal for holiness.
But in time some clergy, drawn to it simply
by a liking for its ceremonial and ritualism,
revived practices which had not been seen for
almost three centuries. Many Anglicans saw these
trends within their own church, together with the
growing emancipation of Roman Catholics, as a
real threat to their Protestant heritage won by
the blood of the Reformation martyrs.

It is against this background of national religious ferment that we must seek to understand
the attitudes and actions of those involved in particular localities. In the 1870s (when anti-Popery
street riots reached their height in London and
elsewhere) a new church was built on the eastern
side of Bournemouth. Under its first incumbent,
an ardent ritualist, it soon gained a reputation
for 'extreme' catholic doctrine and practice. Some
prominent local churchmen were unwilling to tol-
erate this. They petitioned for the formation of a
new parish in Boscombe, its living to be in the
gift of the Peache Trustees, who would ensure a
distinctively evangelical ministry. So St John's
was born: and for almost 100 years it has been
consistently known as 'soundly evangelical'!

The Early Years

Early incumbents were outstanding preachers and pastors, and the building was regularly full. Even before the church building was begun, a cottage in the new parish was acquired and adapted as a mission hall where the 'artisans of the district' and the 'lads and girls who would otherwise roam the streets' could meet for recreation and teaching. We cannot trace here the story of all the people who have laboured at St John's down the years – this book is not a history. But a true picture can be gained of an event or period only through some appreciation of the circumstances leading up to it. Sir Winston Churchill said that a nation which has forgotten its past can have no future. That is true of God's kingdom. As we watch his purposes unfolding, we need to be constantly aware both of our debt to past generations of Christians and of our responsibility to those who will follow us. It is perhaps a particular weakness today that Christians often fail to put their own experience of worship and service in the context of either the past or the future.

A brief backward glance is therefore essential, because any suggestion that the recent events described in this book are a complete story in themselves would be misleading. Worse than that, it would do a serious injustice to previous generations of Christians who have worked and worshipped at St John's. Without their faithfulness, insights and prayers, none of the present developments could have happened. The phase of God's work on which we have entered in the last decade grows in a real sense out of what went before. It

was instructive and humbling to come across a
bookmark carrying a prayer composed by Norman
Bainbridge (Vicar of St John's from 1966 to 1980).
It asked God to make us an effective and united
church by the renewing of his Holy Spirit, and
went on, *enable us by the quality of our lives, by
serving the community in which we live and by
witnessing in other ways, to give positive encouragement to others to turn to you in repentance and
faith.*' No doubt those using it in the 1970s saw
many answers: but how abundantly God has gone
on to answer it now in the 1990s! There is a vital
lesson here – especially perhaps for those engaged
in a 'new' Christian work or, in these days of
church planting, in 'new' (i.e. recently-formed)
fellowships. Nothing is altogether new! We all
need to acknowledge that our work is rooted in
other people's faith and prayer. And we need to
accept that it may be God's will for others to reap
the harvest for which *we* work and pray. (See
1 Corinthians 3: 6, 7, 10.) The key is humility.
Without it we are always liable to regard our own
time, place and work as supremely, if not uniquely,
important. That is a seriously warped perspective on God's kingdom. It is a healthy spiritual
discipline to let the Creed's reference to 'the communion of saints' remind us of this dimension.

The basic priorities set at St John's foundation
may be summed up as,

the faithful preaching of the word and administration of the gospel sacrament in the context of attractive worship;

outreach to those in the area who might not
be regarded as 'natural churchgoers';

an active interest in and support for overseas mission.

Although the particular emphasis on each may have varied from time to time, these have consistently been the keynotes of the first hundred years of the church's life and work.

A Measure of Faithfulness

But consistency in the priorities and style of a church's ministry is not necessarily an indication of consistent 'success'. Perhaps it would be better to use the term 'faithfulness to the gospel', because 'success' is a highly subjective, potentially misleading, and at times extremely dangerous, concept in the realm of spiritual things. It is all too easy to play the numbers game for its own sake. In a slightly different context, I was recently lamenting our lack of success in attracting many people to a recital series I had organised. Someone suggested a simple solution: put on instead evenings of songs from the shows, and people would come flocking in. No doubt they would. Likewise if I promoted boxing matches! But it would not have solved my problem, which was how to attract people to recitals. The parallel is obvious. There *is* a real temptation for the church to play the numbers game, and in so doing forget the business it is in. Many parts of the Church in Britain courted that temptation in the 1960s and 70s, and it would be easy to repeat that mistake in this Decade of Evangelism.

But if numbers are not to be seen as the only, or even main, indicator of a church's faithfulness to the gospel, what other measure might be used? A truer perception may be gained by attempting to assess how closely its ministry matches the needs of the people to whom it is, or should be, ministering. To put it another way, is it 'scratching where people itch'? Of course, a church which is doing that may well attract large numbers: but they are the by-product, not the driving force, of its ministry, a reflection, not a measure, of its faithfulness. Several things need to be said about applying this criterion. The most obvious is that it implies knowledge about the people and their needs, and this is examined in Chapter Five. Secondly, in an ever more rapidly-changing world, people's needs are constantly changing. It is a truism (which also happens to be true!) that they always need Christ and his unchanging gospel: the question is how best to make them aware of that need and Christ's ability to meet it. The answer to that question changes all the time. However we define faithfulness to the gospel, being able to recognise the nature of those changes, and ready to adapt to them, is close to the heart of the matter. Chapter Six reflects further on this. Lastly, this measure (i.e. the match between ministry and needs) is one which can be applied only with the benefit of hindsight. Consequently we ought to apply it to the work of our predecessors with due humility, and hope that those who follow us will look on our own work with equal compassion and understanding.

Church and People 1900–1950

In the first decades of this century the elegant houses on Boscombe's tree-lined avenues were almost new. Their well-to-do occupants attended church with their children in the morning, sending the servants to evening service! Those times were quite unselfconscious about class; it was entirely without her tongue in her cheek that Mrs Alexander attributed the gulf between 'the rich man in his castle' and the 'poor man at his gate' to the benevolence of a God who had ordered it so! So the division of the new parish's worshippers between 'church' and 'mission hall' right from the start need cause us no surprise. Anyway both were almost immediately full to overflowing. Contemporary records suggest that they were highly successful in providing what the people needed.

But the First World War and the depression of the 1920s radically changed many people's outlook. The ordinary man and woman found it harder to accept Browning's assertion 'God's in his heaven, all's right with the world'. Many had lost loved-ones in the horror of the trenches; men had lost their jobs, and now standing in the bread queues they lost their self-respect. The Church faced new challenges as assumptions previously thought sacrosanct were questioned, particularly by young people. St John's worked hard to adapt to this changing society. A parish mission in the early 1930s produced a number of new young Christians. At first the structures were not flexible enough to contain this influx of fresh life, which consequently found outlets for expression in unofficial groups and activities. Frowned on

at first as unwelcome competition to the 'real'
church, this new life was eventually incorporated
under the inspired leadership of the Curate, Max
Warren (subsequently General Secretary of the
Church Missionary Society). The Shelley Road
mission hall gained a new lease of life as 'St
John's Youth Centre', where as Diocesan Youth
Chaplain he ran evening services for youngsters
from neighbouring Anglican churches.

After the Second World War – during which
the hall was requisitioned for military purposes
– evening services were re-started. These were
specially geared to those returning from the war
– St John's again striving to meet the needs of the
time. Meanwhile, worship at the church continued
much as before. But by now the questioning of
Christian belief by ordinary people was being
reinforced by direct attacks on the faith by the
country's intellectuals, and there was a general,
steady decrease in church membership. St John's
was not immune from this, and its life appears to
have been, in some respects, at a low ebb.

1950–1980

But 1951 saw the arrival of Gordon Guinness
as Vicar. An inspiring preacher and teacher,
outstanding pastor and evangelist, he was the
all-rounder most people expect all clergy to be!
He and his wife Grace, who did a great deal
of work amongst women, were a remarkable
team. During the next ten years they saw steady
numerical growth. Communicant numbers nationally increased during the late 50s and early 60s[2];

but growth at St John's was well in excess of this
trend, and its 1,100 seats were once again filled
on occasions. People travelled up to 30 miles to
Morning and Evening Prayer, the large 'Children's Church' and Bible class, and flourishing
organisations for the youth and various other
social - and age-related groupings. Underlying all
this activity was a solid basis of biblical preaching
and teaching and individual pastoral care. Many
members responded to a call to ordination and
overseas mission work. Evangelism was carried
out by open-air missions and in the local cinema,
and the church actively supported social work in
the parish. No wonder there are still those who
look back on those years – not without a touch of
nostalgia – as a heyday.

A number of those who were youngsters at St
John's in the 1950s went on to full-time Christian
ministry. The effects of this rich period spread
far and wide. But some disruptive influences
within the congregation affected the Guinness'
latter years at St John's, and numbers were
already declining. There was a further sharp drop
after they left in 1965. No doubt the reasons for
this are complex; but they certainly include the
fact that this outstanding Christian leader had
a personal following. We often say that someone
is 'a difficult act to follow', and yet this situation
is rarely of their own making. They have simply
employed their gifts faithfully, with total dedication and commitment. Often they may have
actively discouraged this kind of personal following. Yet the frequency with which this phenomenon is observed ought to prompt serious questions about why the ongoing life of a particular

church can be so volatile. I shall touch on this in the next chapter.

Though by the standards of the time St John's was still a large congregation, it is understandable why those who remained felt themselves to be living in the shadow of a great era. This is never an easy atmosphere in which to work and worship. Furthermore, national figures for church *attendance*, which now became available in addition to those for *membership*, showed that a sharp decline set in following the swinging, 'never-had-it-so-good' 60s. Attendance figures in the Church of England between 1968 and 1978 fell by over 22 per cent.[2]

Undaunted, Norman Bainbridge, who had earlier enjoyed a successful ministry as an Army chaplain, came from St James's, Muswell Hill in London, to take up the challenge of becoming Vicar of St John's. He set about his task with great zeal. In the early 1970s St John's had organisations catering for all ages, sound teaching, a systematic approach to parish visiting and a lively interest in overseas mission. He was particularly loved by the children, who would always cluster round him whenever he appeared! Disruptive influences remained, but he took positive action wherever possible to foster a sense of family in the church. For example, he began a series of weekend houseparties at which people started to get to know one another much better. He took care that these included people who were new or on the fringe, often making it possible for some to attend who could otherwise not afford to do so.

A sketch of St John's in the 1950s

Norman Bainbridge, with his wife Sylvia who
began the playgroup which was to become such
a crucial part of St John's work, demonstrated
a great concern for people. He showed that he
really cared. Moreover he was constantly calling
the membership to prayer – though often, it seems,
with not much visible response. Indeed, as he met
with his wardens and other leaders to review
progress and plans for the future, they often felt
that, although there were encouragements, they
were not seeing the results that they 'ought' to
see from so much careful preparation and faithful
work.

But times were changing. The church could no
longer make an impact on the community just by
being there and doing its work faithfully. And
if this was true locally it reflected the general
trend of the Church's position in the nation.
In the 1940s Archbishop William Temple had
put the Church near the centre of national life,
courageously insisting that the gospel's insights
should be brought to bear on the political and
social issues of the day. But after his untimely
death in 1944 it was not long before the voice of
the Church was largely drowned amid the clamour
of competing theories and philosophies. Ordinary
people were encouraged to look to the psychol-
ogists, sociologists and economists for salvation.
But since it is only in retrospect that such broad
trends can be seen for what they are, it is unfair
to be too critical of what may look like slowness
to adapt to changing times.

It is that same benefit of hindsight which enables
us to see how this national trend manifested itself at
the level of individual local churches, particularly in

the towns and cities. There was a gradual loss of
identity with the communities in which they were
located – and for which, in many instances, they
had been built. This was exacerbated by increased
mobility as transport systems improved and car
ownership spread; populations moved outwards
from old town centres; and family ties and loyalty
to a local area were weakened. Instead of being
central to the community's life, churches were
becoming just buildings on the local scene. Their
exterior was still a familiar landmark ('turn left
by the church at the crossroads'), but for increasing numbers of local people what went on inside
was a matter of idle speculation or complete
indifference. At St John's, its members also felt
themselves to be overshadowed by their recent
past. But I believe there was another, potent factor
at work here also. It affects the life of many similar
churches, and it is to this we must now turn.

CHAPTER THREE

GATHERED CONGREGATION OR PARISH CHURCH?

The strengths of a consistent style of ministry in a church over many years are obvious; but it may also contain hidden weaknesses. Such a church usually identifies strongly with a particular tradition of doctrine and practice – probably near one extreme or another! John Henry Newman noted the tendency of some Christians to make *statements* of belief and practice into the *objects* of faith. Commenting on this, Michael Ramsey points out that it is possible to pay more attention to believing in a doctrine than to believing in the Christ to whom it refers.[1] We have seen how the early years of St John's were shaped by the crusading zeal of its founders to provide an antidote to what they saw as the errors of neighbouring parishes. The patronage of the living ensured that future incumbents were all likely to have similar convictions. Naturally the expression of those convictions has varied from one individual to another; but this 'succession' has ensured that the tendency to concentrate on our beliefs *per se* has survived to the present day.

Evidence for this can be found on the noticeboard outside the church. Put up in the early 1980s,

and surviving until very recently, it read 'This
building was opened in 1895. Ever since this date
the ministry and worship of the congregation has
been firmly rooted within the evangelical tradition
of the Church of England.'

As a statement of fact this is unassailable. But
it is, in effect, a coded message, whose intended
significance will be understood in the 1990s by
only a small minority even amongst churchgoers;
99 per cent of passers-by can have not the slightest
idea what it means! I suspect it mainly meets our
own need to say something about ourselves.

If strongly-held convictions are easily elevated
from articles of faith into objects of faith, it is
also true that those with like convictions tend
to congregate at those churches whose ministry bears them out. This reinforces the tendency
still further, producing a cyclical effect. Today's
mobility makes it easy for urban churchgoers
to travel to a church which 'suits' them. Some
Anglican churches have taken on the nature of a
'gathered church', rather than a 'parish church'
whose congregation is predominantly local. This
happens not only to churches, like St John's,
with a strong Bible-based teaching ministry; the
same effect may be seen where any particularly
distinctive style or tradition emerges. It may be
catholic ceremonial, charismatic worship, choral
tradition or adherence to the 1662 Prayer Book.
(I knew a London church to which four people
used to travel 50 miles every Sunday for the
1549 Communion service!) During the next few
years the polarisation arising from the ordination of women will doubtless increase further
this tendency of churchgoers to commute to a

church which reinforces their own convictions or
feelings.

Since the *gathered church* mentality has – as
I shall hope to show – a significant effect on
a church's willingness to engage with the local
community, it is vital to understand the concept if
we are to go on to examine church and community
. . . which is the essence of our recent experiences
at St John's.

Historical Background

The parish system, in something like its present
form, dates from before the Norman conquest.
Until the middle of the seventeenth century everyone was required by law to attend their parish
church weekly. Even when this was relaxed, the
basis of the parish system remained, i.e. that the
soul of everyone in the land was the spiritual
responsibility of a parochial clergyman. So when
the new Church of England was finally established
with the monarch as its Supreme Governor, every
member of the population was, legally-speaking, a
member of the Church. It was literally a *national*
Church.

But this new established Church was not nearly
reformed enough for some. Those who dissented
from it grew in numbers and influence and eventually in 1689 the existence of independent, 'non-
conformist' congregations was legally recognised.
So the *gathered church* as an accepted institution in Britain is only some 300 years old.
Non-conformism has been a significant part of
the scene ever since. Although it is often the

differences over externals – clerical dress, posture and liturgical formulae – which come to mind, there were more fundamental issues which concerned the first independent congregations. They believed strongly in local control of church affairs and appointment of ministers, and wanted nothing to do with church hierarchies and ordination by Bishops. For them, regarding the Church as co-terminous with the nation was a complete anathema. They saw the Church as a body of true Christians called out, or gathered, from society. This produced the very different ethos which persists in non-conformist churches to this day. The 'Free-church' minister has no *legal* responsibility for the care of anyone. He may, if he so chooses, limit his task to the care and nurture of his own gathered flock.

The Position of the Church of England

Not so the Anglican clergyman. He is still legally responsible for the spiritual wellbeing of everyone in his parish. This charge of 'the cure of souls' is laid on him at his institution to a parish. Instituting Godfrey Taylor in 1981, Bishop John Taylor emphasised this strongly. He said the new Vicar would be

> responsible to embody the love of God for every man, woman and child who reside within the boundaries of this parish ... He undertakes – but of course not alone – *you* undertake to live for this community in the

name of Christ. That is the special glory, and
the special task, of the Church of England as
the national Church.

He told the congregation

we are not a sect; you have not just got the new
manager of a religious club. You are something
very much greater than that: you are God's
mission to the whole area of Bournemouth that
is known as St John's . . . a specific neighbourhood that is made your responsibility.

It could not be put more clearly. What he was saying
is at the heart of what it means to be the 'established
Church'. (This remarkably apposite and prophetic
sermon is reproduced in full in the Appendix.)
    Whether or not this ideal is realistic, or indeed
desirable, in today's secular society is a matter for
debate – a debate which is catching the attention
of the media even as I write. But it is important
to understand and remember that, legally at least,
there is this sharp distinction between the position
of the Church of England and all other churches
in Britain. It has a vital bearing on the situation
which arises when an Anglican church becomes
in effect a gathered church for Christians of a
particular tendency within a given area.

A Closed System

When that happens, two factors are at work which
tend to reinforce one another. First, since a large
proportion of the members agree on the matters
which give the church the distinctive character
which attracted them, this consensus encourages

the leadership to see its task in terms of meeting their aspirations. It homes in more and more closely on these features, practising them ever more single-mindedly, so that they become the 'correct' things to do and believe. This tendency to reinforce existing prejudices eventually produces an 'exclusive' outlook. Neighbouring churches with different traditions or priorities begin to seem at best inferior, or at worst wrong; in time they may come to be ignored altogether. That church then exists primarily for its own members, and its minister is in effect a 'chaplain to the faithful'.

Secondly, this exclusive concentration on the interests and insights of its own members dulls its sense of responsibility to the people of its parish. However much *they* may need *it*, the gathered church does not *need* them in the same way as a church whose congregation is mainly local. Because it draws like-minded people from a wide area, its activities and organisations thrive without reference to local people. In some ways it may feel better off without them: after all, they would not have the perceptions required to 'fit in'. This is not to say that it is entirely inward-looking; but its missionary enthusiasm is often directed more towards distant lands than the surrounding streets. There is less danger of any missionary 'success' impinging back onto its own life and activities!

The Body of Christ

These two factors jointly give rise to a 'proprietorial' attitude by some to 'their' church. Is it partly this, I wonder, which makes it so easy for

them to pack up their tents and go elsewhere when
the Vicar says something unpalatable, or when a
particular leader departs? If the congregation had
developed a sense of *corporate* responsibility for
the surrounding community, they could surely not
walk away from it so lightly. Sadly, the evidence
suggests that some apparently well-taught Christians never get beyond seeing a particular church
as there for them to join because they like its style.
The truth never sinks in that by joining it they are
becoming members of the Body of Christ in that
place, and that this has two serious implications:

1) It gives them a responsibility towards
their fellow-members. (See 1 Corinthians
12:12–27; Philippians 2:4.) David Watson
puts it well: 'The church is emphatically *not*
an agglomeration of pious individuals who
happen to believe the same gospel. Certainly
our faith is to be a personal faith; but it is not
to be private.'[2]
2) It commits them to a share in the church's
primary task – to be the agent of God's love in
the world (Matthew 5:13–16 and 28:19–20).
'The calling of God,' writes David Watson,
'is to share sacrificially his love and gifts
with the needy and suffering world around
us. It is God's intention that as his people
we should glorify him in the world. He has
commissioned us to reveal him through our
corporate life as his "own people" to a world
that does not know him.'[3]

The greatest weakness of the gathered church mentality is that it allows, and arguably encourages, an

unhealthy individualism. In an Anglican church this obscures its responsibility towards its parish. And, as Michael Marshall observes: 'Our theological mandate forbids such a sectarian view, and challenges our members to be actively concerned in . . . the world as part of their Christian spirituality.'[4]

It may be thought that I have depicted these characteristics too sharply. I believe not; I speak from experience. When, with my wife Ann, I arrived at St John's in 1987 as Director of Music, we already knew of it as go-ahead, 'soundly-evangelical' and widely-known for its Bible-based teaching ministry. Happily, we found all of this to be true. But we also came across deeply-entrenched attitudes at which we were taken aback. Some early impressions are still etched on the memory. For instance, soon after our arrival we were told, 'Of course, all the other churches in the area are completely dead' – and the comment was made in all seriousness. Then there was the housegroup meeting at which I voiced my anxiety that we did not seem to be very concerned about our own parish – half the group claimed not to know that we had a 'parish', while one or two (admittedly from Free-church backgrounds) seemed quite unable even to grasp the concept!

I do not want to labour the point needlessly. I have said enough to support the contention that some Anglican congregations think and behave as a *gathered* rather than a *parish* church. I am sure it is no accident that so many former nonconformist Christians have settled at St John's! This self-reinforcing cycle can occur equally within the Anglo-Catholic camp. And the more

recently-formed charismatic fellowships (sometimes mainly gathered out of the other churches!)
can become afflicted with an exclusive mentality,
prompting them to dismiss as 'not Spirit-filled'
those whose understanding and experience differ
from their own.

Neither do I want to sound too judgmental.
Whatever their legal responsibilities, in practice
some Anglican clergy exhibit no 'zeal for souls' in
relation to their parishioners; while many Free-
church pastors, with no such legal responsibilities,
are deeply and actively concerned for all the people
of their locality. Some might argue, with good
reason, that it is these actual facts, rather than
the theory, which matter.

Scriptural Background

The Bible contains remarkably little explicit teaching about 'the Church': and it is wise to be
cautious in our exegesis of its underlying themes
about the 'people of God'. But those looking for
Scriptural support for one 'model' or the other will
find, on a balanced reading, that both ideas are
present. One group of ideas supports the concept
of the Church as a minority called into existence
from society at large. The 'righteous remnant' of
the Old Testament, corresponding with the 'invis-
ible Church', is succeeded in the New Testament
by the 'little flock' of God's people called out to
be separate from the world. Conversely the Old
Testament makes clear that the whole of Israel,
however unfaithful, were still God's covenant
people, with a responsibility to witness to his glory

among the nations. So in the New Testament those who are *called* and *chosen* are also *sent*: and the Church (the 'New Israel') has a perpetual responsibility in and to the world of which it is a part.

These two strands of thought – and space forbids me to develop them in more detail here – need to be held in tension to maintain a balanced view of the Church in the world.[5] To identify the Church automatically with the nation is clearly untenable today. Conversely, it is unacceptable to retreat into a sheltered enclave, adopting a mentality which allows us to regard as the true Church only those shut in with us and speaking the same language. God's people have the responsibility of proclamation, intercession and service in the world.

Implications for the Parish Church

The reflections in this chapter are not intended to be polemical or partisan. They draw attention to the fact that, although continuity in a church's style of ministry can build up a strong fellowship and provide a consistent witness to particular aspects of God's truth, the 'gathered church' mentality brings with it, especially in the Parish church context, concomitant dangers. These are very real; yet they are seldom recognised – especially by the members of such churches, who are simply too close to be able to see them. Ironically, this very mentality discourages them from going elsewhere and enabling them to see it for what it is!

I suggested in Chapter 2 that one yardstick by which to measure faithfulness to the gospel is the

extent to which a church is meeting the needs
not only of those to whom it is ministering, but
also of those to whom it *ought to be* ministering.
Churches which have stood proudly for one particular tradition for many generations are often
less faithful in the second of these two aspects
than the first. There have been times when St
John's, while numerically strong and meeting its
members' needs, has nevertheless been essentially
inward-looking. Although many people came into
the building on Sundays, their presence had little
discernible effect on the local community, of which
they themselves had scant knowledge. Many never
gave the parish a thought. For an Anglican church
this must be seen as failing in an important part of
its ministry. No *parish* church has a mandate for
opting out of its responsibility to the people of its
parish in favour of its gathered members or, indeed,
of mission fields in more distant places.

And yet churches in this phase can appear lively
and successful. They may have respected leaders and satisfied followers. They may be happy
and united fellowships, secure in their common
conviction that theirs is the authentic brand of
Christianity. The people come Sunday by Sunday
and get what they like. In token of this, they may
give reasonably generously, so that their church
is able to maintain and even expand the style of
ministry to which they have become accustomed.
Who could ask for more?

God could. And does. He asks that we grow
beyond that.

CHAPTER FOUR

GROWING FROM THE CENTRE

'There is a time to plant and a time to uproot ... a time to tear down and a time to build' (Ecclesiastes 3:2–3). These processes, the apparently negative as well as the obviously positive ones, are all involved in growth. Examples are all around us. In the garden I prune roses and cut herbaceous perennials down to the ground to promote strong, healthy new growth. On a building site, anything already there must be demolished before construction can begin. Removing the old so that something new may grow is commonplace. But it is not a universal principle: although pruning makes my roses grow, it would not do to apply the same treatment to my children! So there is also 'a time to keep and a time to throw away' (Ecclesiastes 3:6). Some things must be kept, because another kind of growth involves nurturing what exists. Growth is a varied and complex process, often unpredictable, sometimes risky. And it always involves change.

All this is true of growth within a church. I do not mean growth in numbers, but in effective service and witness, in corporate as well as individual maturity ... spiritual growing up.

An adolescent provides some instructive parallels
– perhaps we ought to expect someone returning
to our church after a time away to exclaim like a
fond aunt, 'How you've grown!' As a youth grows
in fits and starts through the release of hormones,
so the church may experience spurts of growth
punctuated by apparently static periods as the
Holy Spirit 'blows wherever he pleases'. This is
perfectly normal; but no growth at all over an
extended period indicates something organically
wrong. At times in a growing church the Body
may seem awkward and gangly, like a youngster
who is all arms and legs. The Corinthians were in
this phase when Paul wrote to them – growing in
a vigorous but unco-ordinated way, leaving them
unbalanced and often tripping up. Some teenagers
go through a 'bookish' stage, when they seem of no
real use to anyone, though in fact they are storing
up knowledge which will be of immense value
later. Similarly, there may be phases when a growing church appears to be learning rather than producing, but which can later be seen as necessary
preparation for some new outreach or service.

Growth is essentially a long-term process. A
snapshot of a church at one point in time will
rarely, if ever, give a true impression of what is
actually going on. This can be discovered only over
a period of time. Resist the temptation to make a
snap judgement about that church you visit while
on holiday – or, indeed, too hastily about your own!

God's Time – God's Man

St John's was poised for a burst of dramatic
growth at the beginning of the 1980s. Much prayer

and faithful work had been going on for some
years. The right time for growth had arrived: now
it needed the right person to spark it off. The
churchwardens felt with overpowering certainty
that Godfrey Taylor was the man of God's choice.
It is significant that the hallmark of his ministry
had been stimulating growth through change. To
appreciate the story of what was to come at St
John's, it is necessary to sketch in a little of his
background.

Brought up in the Medway towns in Kent during
the Second World War, Godfrey was converted at
the age of 18. After a short spell as a teacher
he followed up a call to the ministry, study-
ing at Oakhill theological college. In his first
curacy, on the North Kent coast, he soon found
himself unexpectedly in charge of the parish.
This fuelled that independence which is a major
part of his make-up; so it was fortunate that his
second curacy in the large parish of St James',
Tunbridge Wells involved starting a new Family
Service from scratch in a school on a housing
estate. Without the injection of resources and
manpower which would launch a 'church plant'
today, Godfrey and his wife Daphne saw this new
congregation grow to almost 200 before they left
in 1968.

It was a big leap from there to his first living
as Vicar of Holy Trinity, Guernsey. In 13 years
there he oversaw a number of changes leading to
a growth in work amongst young people, dramati-
cally altering the age-profile of the congregation.
Many of these youngsters have now married and
are raising families within the fellowship of the
church. Changes to the building planned in his

final year have since been carried out. The Channel Islands are a part of the Diocese of Winchester; but the five hour boat trip between them and the mother church inevitably lends a certain feeling of detachment not unattractive to a man of independent spirit! The Taylors found their ministry there very fulfilling, and their four children, three of whom were born in Guernsey, made many friends on the island. Leaving was a real wrench for them all.

But it was time to go. It was not just the innate restlessness of the man: he had a strong sense of God's call to St John's, Boscombe. He knew its history and reputation; and its strong biblical tradition was one with which he was not only entirely in sympathy, but for which his own gifts as a Bible expositor equipped him. It was in many ways a natural progression. He was not to know then that this move would, in due course, present him with challenges to personal change and growth as great as any which he had delivered to others!

Church and Community

By comparison with Guernsey, Boscombe lacked a feeling of community. It 'had no heart'. Although in villages life often still centred around the church, in towns it was 20 or 30 years since most churches had begun to lose their foothold in the community. Could a church like St John's ever regain that position? And should it? It was, as we have noted, the mentality of the 'gathered' church – focussed on the membership rather than the parish – which had shaped the congregation's thinking for many years . . . an outlook with which their new Vicar could easily identify. Nevertheless, he had been given a specific charge by the Bishop of Winchester at his institution to look outwards, and lead his congregation in being the embodiment of God's love 'to every man, woman and child in the parish'. His starting point would be to update the church's ministry, to make it as relevant as possible at least to the whole spectrum of members.

St John's had a variety of buildings. Next to the church was the Selwyn Hall, a large barn-like structure from the 1890s. There was a former church school, closed some years previously. Half a mile from the church stood the 'St John's Halls', a Victorian cottage with a hall added in 1910; this had for many years served as a mission hall, but since the 1950s had been used almost exclusively by the Boys' Brigade company. How could these assets be developed to advance the church's ministry? Decisions deferred pending his arrival now urgently needed to be taken

The school site had limited potential, and was in an area scheduled for redevelopment. The Selwyn Hall was inflexible and showing its age. Anyway, he foresaw growth in activity, particularly among youngsters, which could not all be accommodated on the one site. Attention focussed on the St John's Halls. The cottage was fit only for demolition, and the rest was very run down. To do anything worthwhile would be a major project. The PCC discussed various ideas and in December 1982 a proposed development was put to a special church meeting.

Seeing People Through Buildings

The story of the next decade can be summed up in
the phrase 'seeing *people* through *buildings*'. In
1982, the main service was Morning Prayer, with
a 'Children's Church' meeting simultaneously in
the Selwyn Hall, the parents coming into church
for the sermon, while the children had their own
classes. Under-5s met upstairs; a 12–15 group had
been hived off to the St John's Halls in Shelley
Road – mainly girls, because the Boys' Brigade
had their own separate meeting. A more integrated
pattern was needed. Complete redevelopment of
the St John's Halls could create the opportunity
to achieve this, and provide young people's groups
with a place for midweek activities. There could be
a church office and rooms for smaller meetings.
In short, a major redevelopment would improve
our ministry to our members – and that would
be its primary purpose. But who could tell how
things might develop? The existing small, part-
time playgroup might be developed into a full-time
community facility. With a new kitchen and dining
area we might provide pensioners' lunches. Godfrey
stressed that not all the detail could be spelt out at
the beginning. This was another lesson which was
to be repeated as the 1980s and 90s unfolded. As
a congregation we have stepped out in a particular
direction in faith, convinced that it is God's will for
us to do so; but only *after* the event have we been
able to recognise the full significance and potential
of what we have done. This lesson in faith does not
seem to come any easier each time we are confronted
with the need for a decision.

How would such an ambitious project be funded?

The congregation must not expect to live on the
financial or spiritual capital of past generations.
The call was to us, the church of today. We were
called to demonstrate real concern for the advance
of God's kingdom by giving sacrificially, over and
above our support for the existing ministry. It was
a big challenge. Many of the more elderly members
(and they were a considerable proportion!) had not
been near the St John's Halls for years; it cannot
have been easy for them to identify with what was
proposed. At first it looked as if the response might
be lukewarm. Undeterred, the Church Council
drew up a detailed scheme at an estimated cost
of around £270,000 – a lot of money in 1983!

The New St John's Centre

A Promise Day and subsequent gifts yielded just
under half that amount. It was decided to go ahead
in faith – a course vindicated when a charitable
trust devoted to local Christian purposes later
offered an outright gift of £27,000 and an interest-
free loan of £100,000. This was joyfully received as
a sign that God was honouring our obedience to
his call by providing from his limitless resources
– not for our gratification, but to enable us to
serve him more effectively. This gave an enormous
fillip to the confidence of the congregation, who
responded with another £34,000. The building
opened in September 1985 entirely free of debt.
The tremendous stimulus to faith which this gave
was to have significant consequences over the next
few years.

The new St John's Centre was dedicated by

Bishop Deqhani Tafti, Assistant Bishop in the
Diocese of Winchester in exile from Iran. Bishop
Oliver Allison, a former curate of St John's, prayed
that the Centre 'may be a place of blessing in
body and spirit to all who use it, so that it may
always be a place where people meet with Jesus
and acknowledge him as Lord'. Today we can look
back and acknowledge with gratitude how richly
God has answered that prayer, and continues to
answer it daily.

Getting Started

We now had our new Centre – how should we
use it? A priority must be to break out of the
limitations of the former 'Children's Church'.
But as Godfrey had seen the building alterations
taking shape he had realised that we should
now have the facilities to develop genuine all-
age worship – a long-felt ambition of his. This
would need more people than ever before to be
actively involved in teaching. Potential leaders
were 'talent-spotted', a move which had the long-
term effect of broadening the base of our teaching
resources. A new music group was formed. The
concept of 'every-member ministry' started to
become an exciting reality; and as more people
became not just involved, but committed, a process of deepening began which has benefited many
areas of the church's life. Today there are over 30
people involved in teaching or leading worship at
the Centre.

If this all sounds easy, nothing could be further
from the truth. Not everyone saw or accepted

the need for change. Some regarded it as split-
ting the church into two, and in a sense it was.
Although the new pattern included a monthly
Family Service for all in the church, the sense
of loss remained. There have been other occasions
where one part of the church family has had to
make a sacrifice for the good of other members or,
as time went by, of those on the fringe or outside.
It is a lesson we shall have to put into practice
repeatedly.

Is this the point at which potential for growth in
many churches is nipped in the bud? People say,
'We like things the way they are. Why change
them just to please some newcomers, let alone
outsiders? If *they* want to join *our* church, let
them adapt to what we do.' This is especially
common where patterns of activity and worship
have long remained undisturbed. It is particularly
noteworthy that it was mainly the older members
of St John's who were called on to make the first
obvious sacrifice as the church began to change
direction. It is a great tribute to their grace and
spiritual maturity that they have come through it,
and most can now recognise the real advances it
has made possible. They are an example to us all:
and it is highly significant that morning worship
at the parish church, which some thought might
dwindle or even die, continues to flourish and has
real spiritual life and depth.

Meanwhile, at the new Centre the youngsters
went straight into their groups on arrival for age-
related teaching/activities on a common theme,
while the adults had their own worship and sermon in the main hall. Afterwards everybody came
together for a short act of all-age worship. Two

aspects of the groups caused concern. First, imbalances and gaps in the age structure made it difficult to allocate teaching resources sensibly at the outset. Secondly, the Boys' Brigade was detached from the mainstream of the church's life, a position which some of its leaders were reluctant to abandon. If a coherent strategy was to be pursued for nurturing our youngsters both in faith and church membership, these problems had to be tackled together with realism and understanding.

It was decided to focus on a new mixed-sex group for the 11s and 12s, moving them on in subsequent years into a new CYFA (Christian Youth Fellowships Association) group. This meant leaving the existing small Pathfinder group, and separate Boys' Brigade groups, to die out by natural wastage as those coming from below were fed into the new mixed-sex groups.

Sadly, this latter proposal proved very contentious, and loyalties were severely tested and strained, including amongst some senior and respected men in the congregation whose own early Christian growth had been in the context of the Brigade, or who had given many years of service as leaders. In addition to our new overall strategy for youngsters' teaching on Sundays, there were other issues. The Brigade, which had in practice had exclusive use of the old St John's Halls for some years, would need to adapt to sharing the new premises with the other groups. The appropriateness of uniformed organisations and military-style hierarchy to the Church of the 1980s was questionable. The strength of the organisation's presence tended to produce competition for the youngsters' loyalties between it and the church – a problem not unknown with other young people's organisations. Matters came to a head in 1987, and the Brigade company left and became attached to another church, taking with it a number of families. There was some bitterness and disillusionment, and an unhappy period ensued. The wounds took many months – in some cases years – to heal. Looking back, we can only account it a necessary step to have taken, but it remains a cause for sadness that so much anguish and hurt were involved.

The Playgroup

Then something happened which later proved to have been the start of a major step forward in our relationship with the local community. A small playgroup had existed for some years on a restricted, part-time basis which meant that it was not subject to 'official' control. Some aspects of this gave rise to concern. Godfrey turned for advice to someone who was to play a crucial role in turning St John's outward to the community. Julie Maddams and her family were already active members of St John's. She had run a playgroup elsewhere in Bournemouth as a commercial venture with a friend, but recently had sold her interest in it. As she thought and prayed, she became convinced that God was calling her not just to advise, but to help. This was definitely not wishful thinking – she had been looking forward to a 'quiet life' as a wife and mother! Nevertheless, she felt so sure that this was a call from God that she said, 'I'll help'.

Her expertise, and the contacts and trust she
had already built up with the social services and
other local agencies, proved invaluable, and she
soon emerged as the natural leader for a new,
fully-registered group, meeting every morning.
From the outset it was made clear that the group
was run on Christian principles and the children would be told about God's love for them
in Jesus. Parents seem to accept this without
demur. Indeed, they often ask Julie or her helpers
questions about Christian things – ostensibly for
their children, but actually because for some it is
on this level that they can take it in for themselves.
Some, having become used to bringing their child
to the Centre, seem willing to do so on Sunday
mornings. A few of the parents may then stay for
all-age worship themselves, provided that one of
the helpers or Christian parents they have got to
know during the week sits with them. Some have
found faith this way.

The playgroup meets a real social need *in the
neighbourhood*: and by doing so unambiguously in
the name of God's Church it is, in the fullest sense,
performing an act of Christian service. Julie has
become well-known, trusted (and indeed loved)
for what she does for a growing circle of local
people, many of them single parents. They know
she is doing it in the church's name. St John's, as
embodied in the Centre, has started once again to
be at the heart of their community. You have only
to try to cut your way through the throng in the
doorway when they come to pick up their children
at midday to see and hear that! But its Christian
impact on the local community goes beyond that.
Julie has taken on as playgroup helpers young

adults from local 'halfway houses' – places where
they are on their way back into society after intensive treatment for alcohol or drug addiction. This
helps their rehabilitation, and also brings them
too within the influence of God's Church.

Ever-Widening Circles

At the outset Godfrey had said that we should not
expect to see, straight away, all the Centre's possible future uses. How right he was! By the time it
opened the vision for all-age worship, which has
since become one of the distinctive hallmarks of
St John's ministry, had been received, developed
and implemented. Within three years the Centre
was a hive of activity six days a week. In addition
to the church's use it became the venue for a
single-parent support group and later a toy library
– activities not run by us but located there by the
social services as a result of their contacts with
us. In one way or another our facilities were being
used to meet urgent local needs. Here was the
Bishop's charge to be 'the embodiment of God's
love in the local community' becoming a tangible
reality.

At the Centre we are at least starting to 'scratch
where people itch'. Many people today – especially those who have got themselves into the
kind of socially-stigmatised categories that many
Boscombe residents have – will not darken the
doors of a church. In opening the Centre as a
place of activity, community service *and* worship
we have, almost unwittingly, created a real worshipping community accessible to such people.

The same thing could never have been achieved
by staying within our grey stone walls and seeking
to bring such people to services – even 'brighter'
services! They came because we had got alongside
to *serve* them, their children, their husbands or
wives. A survey in 1990/91 found that more people
come to faith by personal contact with Christians
in their families or amongst their friends, than in
any other way.[1] We acknowledge with gratitude
that it is God who has enabled us to identify
more closely with the needs of local people, and
has given us the material and human resources
to start trying to meet those needs.

Lessons In Growing

This chapter began by noting some characteristics of spiritual growth. It is appropriate to end
by asking what lessons we had learnt from the
growth that came about through the opening of the
Centre. How had the development of a ministry
there helped lead us on towards the next stages
of growth? And are there general principles here
which may help others to grow? Three main things
appear to be prerequisite for spiritual growth:

   Faith. We have witnessed the kind of growth
– for example in our young people's work – which
could not have taken place without first cutting
down something else. We have also seen the
growth which comes from nurturing what already
exists – the development of our teaching resources.
Both types of growth call for faith, at the outset
and to carry on through the pain. So does the

unpredictability of growth; we had no idea at the
start how God's work at the Centre would take off.
Sticking with what has been started needs faith in
the God who 'knows the end from the beginning'
(Isaiah 46:10).

Obedience. Individually and corporately we
must be ready to seek God's will and follow
it. God has taken our obedience and used it
to do something more than we could ever have
envisaged; this ought to discourage us from being
too prescriptive in our future planning. Obedience
almost always means saying 'no' at some point to
our own inclinations.

Sacrifice. Somewhere along the line obedience always involves sacrifice. Jesus' call to 'take
up your cross, deny yourself, and follow me' is
neither selective nor optional, but universal and
binding. It is the response required of *anyone* serious about discipleship. (See e.g. Luke 9:23–24.)
The implications of this are unmistakable however
much we may try (and we do!) to wriggle out of
them. Generally speaking – though generalisa-
tions always do injustice to some – our own
experience has shown that the greatest losses and
hurts have been both caused by, and suffered by,
those who were unwilling to meet the sacrificial
cost of obedience.

The commonest cause of 'nil growth syndrome',
individually and corporately, is failure to face up
to the cost of obedience. We were beginning to
discover how, when it is faced, it can spur all
kinds of growth. The older folk at the church

made a sacrifice when the Centre was opened on
Sunday mornings. Julie Maddams (who, of all
people, would not want to be portrayed as a
heroine) has been used in a crucial way because
she was willing to sacrifice her own plans when
she heard God's call. In that respect she typifies
others we shall meet as the story unfolds, whose
simple obedience is enabling us to start seeing the
reality of what it means to 'embody the love of God
. . . in this community' (see the Appendix).

But this was only a beginning. Growth, as
we also observed at the start of this chapter,
always involves change, and there was plenty
more to come! Godfrey Taylor is nothing if not a
pioneer. While many of us were busy sorting out
the details of the new Centre, getting it up and
running, becoming excited at the way things were
developing, he was already out in front, sensing a
call from God to do something else.

CHAPTER FIVE

WE JUST WANT TO GET THE FACTS

It was in autumn 1985 that *Faith in the City*, the report of the Archbishop of Canterbury's Commission on Urban Priority Areas, burst on a not-altogether-unsuspecting world, its main thrust having (as now seems customary) been leaked shortly before publication. I suppose a 'Runcie raps Thatcher' headline was just too exciting to keep for another 24 hours! Its general conclusion – which will not have surprised many observers – was that, since the Government's 1977 policy initiative to improve life in the inner cities, conditions had actually worsened. The Commission were 'deeply disturbed' by what they had seen and heard during their visits to Urban Priority Areas (UPAs). But what has this to do with Bournemouth? Everyone knows that this part of the South is a 'green and pleasant land'. A survey not long ago named Winchester as the most comfortably-off town in the country, and its diocese is charmingly rural.

The report called for a national system to be set up which would identify UPA parishes and rank them in order of social deprivation, using the statistical indices officially developed

for that purpose relating to unemployment levels,
overcrowded housing or accommodation lacking
basic amenities, numbers of pensioners living
alone and proportion of single parent households.[1]
The Church of England acted on this. When the
Winchester Diocese's analysis was published it
revealed that Boscombe, particularly the area
covered by St John's parish, was classified as a
UPA, ranking high on the deprivation scale. This
may have surprised many people. It certainly did
most of the congregation who come into St John's
from other areas of the town, and whose only
impressions were gained from the car, on the
seafront, or in the new shopping precinct.

The report also recommended that churches in
UPAs should carry out an 'Audit for the Local
Church', enabling them to get an accurate picture
of the *parish* and its people, and set this alongside
facts about the church's *congregation*, activities,
buildings and finance. This information should
then be used to 'reflect on how at present the
church engages with the realities of life in its
area' and lead to 'decisions being reached about
priorities for action'. A suggested format was provided, with advice on how to go about it.[2]

So it came about that we conducted an audit
at St John's. It proved very important – hence
a whole chapter devoted to it. It produced hard
facts, rather than mere impressions, about the
people of our parish ... where they lived, what
they did, their aspirations and opinions – even
what they thought about us! You do not have to
be in a UPA to realise the importance and value
of such information. *There can be no church with
mission anywhere on its agenda – and surely all*

*churches ought to have – which would not benefit
greatly from such an exercise.*

All of which might lead you to assume that the
Church of the Open Door, of which we saw a
glimpse in Chapter One, was St John's response
to the needs revealed by the audit. It would be nice
to be able to tell the story that way . . . that we got
straight on with it, collected our data, discussed
what action was needed and then set up the
Church of the Open Door to offer help to the
needy of Boscombe. That is the way any well-run
organisation would go about things: research –
planning – action. But, unfortunately, it would
not be true! In fact, we took some time to get
round to an audit. When we did, it was too late to
shape the action we took; but it did very strongly
confirm the need for the work we were about to
start.

Without seeking to make a general excuse for
the church not being businesslike (and often it
is not!) I do not believe this back-to-frontness
mattered. Although Christians know that God
operates in the eternal realm – he 'inhabits eternity' as Isaiah expresses it – it is still hard not
to project onto him our own limitations of time
and space. When we do that we not only fail to
understand the way he works, but we also miss out
on much of the excitement of being his children.
The fact that our audit came after, rather than
before, the laying of our plans for the Church of
the Open Door, does not mean that the two were
not connected in God's economy. The Holy Spirit
was undoubtedly leading our thoughts and actions
throughout both exercises.

The people with whom we had already started

to come into contact at the St John's Centre had brought us up sharply against the social need in our area. Even so our eyes were only half open. There were two reasons for this. First, comparatively few church members knew about it, mainly those at the cutting edge of work at the Centre. Only 1 in 10 church members lived in the parish, and most of the rest who drove to St John's from other areas remained largely unaware of the parish and its inhabitants.

Secondly, even those who were coming into contact with the real social need around us had little idea of its extent. They simply did their best to respond to the individual cases which came their way.

We needed to know more. The weekly staff meeting discussed at length the guidelines for carrying out an audit. In June 1988 a presentation was made to the PCC, who agreed an audit should be undertaken. It would need someone with real conviction about it to lead a planning committee, recruit a team of interviewers and oversee the whole exercise. A pregnant silence descended. It was late at night; we were all tired; someone suggested putting it on the agenda for next month. We did, and for the next month, and the month after that! To those familiar with PCCs this may sound nothing unusual. But for us, it was; generally we either made progress with something or dropped it altogether. The summer came and went, and as autumn dragged into winter Godfrey began to show signs of impatience. In December the PCC heard that a church member had been found who was willing to chair an audit committee. This was at least a start. We committed ourselves to pray about the membership of the rest of the audit team.

At the same meeting the Council agreed to the appointment of a temporary Pastoral Assistant from January until September of the following year. Simon Butler was a very able young man with previous close connections with St John's. A graduate of the University of East Anglia, he had taken a commission in the Royal Navy, but while there had explored a call to the ordained ministry. The Navy's response was to tell him that he was no longer required to complete his commission. This left him with several months to spare before taking up his place at St John's College, Nottingham in October 1989. On arriving he discussed how his secondment could bring maximum benefit to the church and himself. It quickly transpired that playing a major part in the proposed audit would contribute on both counts.

Again the man of God's choosing had arrived to do the job waiting to be done. It had always been clear that certain conditions would have to be met if the audit was ever to get off the ground. The impetus must come from someone who was not only convinced of its worth, but also capable in administration and the handling of masses of detail; able to lead and enthuse a team of interviewers working against a timetable; and, above all, be available to devote a significant amount of their time to it for some months. We had simply not been able to see anyone who fulfilled all these criteria – especially the last! We prayed – God answered, though not from any of the directions in which we had been looking. But we had to wait;

and, as things turned out, we were glad we had
waited. Under the wise chairmanship of a senior
church member a small Audit Committee of half a
dozen people was set up. Simon, as the chief 'doer',
brought a combination of youthful enthusiasm and
administrative flair. It was he who would pull the
results together into a report. By the early weeks
of 1989 the operation was under way.

Preparatory Groundwork

The team first gathered relevant statistical and
geographical information available from public
sources such as the population census,[3] the electoral register and large-scale maps of the area.
This enabled them to build up a house-by-house
picture and plot the function of all the other
buildings in the parish. This preliminary exercise
gave the team a feel for the size of their task,
and, although ours is a small parish, it was fairly
daunting.

The next stage was to collect data directly relevant to our purpose. Three questionnaires were
drawn up to gather

- basic information from a sample of parishioners;
- similar information from members of the
  congregation;
- more qualitative and reflective responses
  from forty selected church members.

Before any of these were sent out, leaflets were
distributed in the parish and to church members

telling them what was going on and asking for their help.

The Parish Questionnaire

The parish questionnaire was in two parts. The first aimed to collect factual data about age, sex, marital status, employment, housing, length of time in the area and so on. The second sought parishioners' opinions on the area (likes/dislikes, problems etc.) and their views of/contacts with the church and the Christian faith. The team visited in pairs, in some cases leaving the questionnaire and in others completing it during their visit. They generally received a positive welcome; residents were 'glad that the church was going out to the people'. Over 200 questionnaires were completed, representing almost 10 per cent of the population of the parish. The size of the sample, and the fact that they were carefully selected in different parts of the parish and in different types of housing, justifies a high degree of confidence in the representative nature of the responses.

The Results

Within the parish there were 173 business premises, four other places of worship, five pubs and one night club, a bail hostel and no schools. More significantly, the number of 'visitors' places', i.e. beds in hotels and guest houses, exceeded the 2,700 permanent residents. Some of the key facts about these were:

- over 70 per cent lived in rented accommodation;
- 25 per cent of all households in this part
  of Boscombe were living in one room;
- over half the people surveyed had lived in
  Boscombe for less than five years;
- 57 per cent were single, divorced, sepa-
  rated or widowed (we decided not to press
  the remaining 43 per cent on whether they
  were married to their partner, but anec-
  dotal evidence suggests that a significant
  proportion were not);
- around half of those in work were in
  manual/clerical occupations. (The 42 per
  cent claiming to be 'managerial/profes-
  sional' were treated with caution after
  a bus driver described himself as 'professional' – as an occasional passenger,
  I hope they all are ... but that was not
  quite what we meant!);
- 45% owned a car.

Of the parishioners 43 per cent said they 'practised
some religion', though it was not always entirely
clear what they meant! 67 per cent claimed to have
had some contact with the Church (20 per cent
no denomination mentioned, 15 per cent Church
of England, 7 per cent Roman Catholic, 2 per
cent non-conformists, 2 per cent Jewish), some
admitting this was only at baptisms, weddings,
funerals, or in their childhood. The main dislikes
about Boscombe were crime, vandalism, drink and
traffic. Race relations did not arise (only 7 per cent
of the local population originate from overseas),
but a strong dislike of Liverpudlians, many of

whom come to the area seeking seasonal work, emerged more than once. The majority thought there was little or nothing the local church could do to alleviate social problems. Amongst the more positive minority the most common suggestion was to provide a meeting place – the words 'open door' were actually used. The sample included some members of other churches; a number of these expressed sadness that St John's was not involved in the Boscombe ecumenical scene.

The Congregational Questionnaire

The congregational questionnaire covered similar ground. Again, just over 200 were completed –

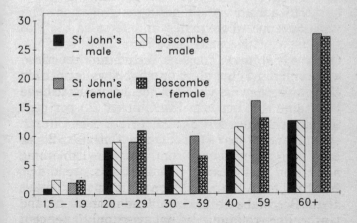

Table 1: Age Distribution
Source: 1981 Census figures for Boscombe West area. 1989 Parish Audit sample (approx 50%) of members.

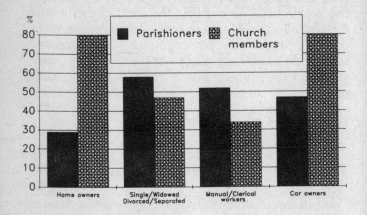

Table 2: Comparison of personal circumstances
Source: 1989 Parish Audit

by no means the whole adult congregation. The imbalance between males and females did not surprise us (the usual 'Lord here am I, send my sister' syndrome). The age distribution of those who completed questionnaires is shown (see Table 1), compared with that for the whole Boscombe West area (1981 census). Take heart: it is not just the church which is full of elderly ladies!

Comparing the results of the two questionnaires highlighted some sharp contrasts (see Table 2).

We collected church attendance figures, but various factors, especially the opening of the St John's Centre in 1985, complicated those for the mornings. Numbers at evening services had shown a steady drop from 156 in 1985 to 103 in 1988, but then steadied and appeared to be increasing

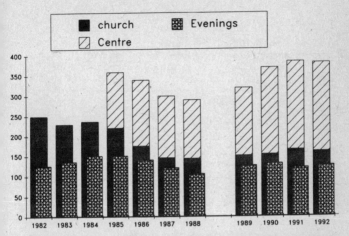

Source: 1989 Parish Audit   Source: Membership Records

Table 3: Average attendance at Sunday services

NOTES:
1)   St John's Centre opened September 1985: figures
prior to that do NOT include those children already
meeting separately from adults at the church.
2)   Figures for morning services at the church include
all-age worship on 1st Sunday of each month and major
festivals: average attendance on other Sundays is therefore
somewhat below the figures shown.

slightly at the time of the audit. (See Table 3
which, for general interest, has been updated to
show a further four years beyond the audit's 1988
cut-off.)

   The facts about financial giving were an encouragement. Income from giving (including tax relief
on covenants) increased from around £240 per
week in 1979 to £850 in 1988. In real terms (i.e.
after allowing for inflation) this represented an

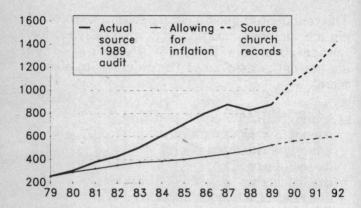

Table 4: Amount given per week

increase of 175 per cent. When falling membership throughout the same period is taken into account, this reflects a considerable increase in giving per member. Moreover these figures relate only to 'regular' giving; they do not include the substantial extra giving towards such major capital projects as the St John's Centre. Table 4 shows these, and has been updated to 1992.

This all added up to a picture of a congregation which, compared with the people living in the parish, was predominantly family-based, middle-class and well-off. Although this came as no surprise, seeing the hard facts in print brought home to us the vast culture and lifestyle gap between those who come to St John's on Sundays and those living around the church. This glimpse of life in the local community was significant for planning.

Confidential Questionnaire

The confidential questionnaire sent to 40 selected church members sought more qualitative information about how they saw St John's. The top six strengths mentioned (in order of frequency) were:

sound, biblically-based teaching
friendly, welcoming fellowship
a family-orientated church
its social caring
the leadership and vision of the clergy
diversity of music in worship.

The top six perceived weaknesses were:

lack of ecumenical involvement
a tendency to individualism
spread over two separate sites
lack of lay leadership
lack of freedom in worship
inadequate regular, corporate prayer.

These responses were of considerable interest. It was surprising to see 'social caring' already listed as a strength in early 1989. From today's vantage point we would say that we had hardly begun to work in that area. (It may be, of course, that some of the respondents were thinking of it within the context of the church family.) It was also notable to find a feeling of being cut off from valuable contact with other churches top of the list of weaknesses, especially as it mirrored the comments made to

the team by Christians of other denominations
living in the parish. The individualism to which
I have already referred as an inherent weakness
was also perceived by members to dilute the corporate life which ought to exist. The comment about
lack of lay leadership gave pause for thought.

Recommendations for Action

Arising from the mass of information which we
now had – and of which this is only the scantiest
summary – the Audit Committee made seven
recommendations. These were:

1. The PCC should form a sub-committee to plan
a strategy for mission and evangelism, bearing
in mind the principal points to emerge from the
audit.
2. We ought to give serious thought to greater
involvement with other local churches.
3. Attempts should be made to counteract individualism and introspection by placing deliberate
emphasis in teaching and church life generally
on our mutual responsibility as fellow-members
of Christ's Body.
4. Any plans made concerning the future of the
Selwyn Hall should take note of the perceived need
for a meeting-place in Boscombe.
5. Arrangements should be made to up-date the
information contained in the audit, in particular
after the 1991 census figures were published.
6. All those involved in planning and leading
worship should be alert to the importance of our
services being amenable to those living in the area.

In addition, the ministry needed to be undergirded
by greater commitment to corporate prayer.
7.   Attention should be paid to improving com-
munications throughout our church life.

It would not be right to let the findings of an
audit set a rigid agenda for the foreseeable future.
Nevertheless the true value of such an exercise
begins to be realised only when it issues in a
definite action plan. The story of how St John's
has developed its life and ministry since 1989, and
where we think we are going at the time of writing,
forms the remainder of this book. You may judge
for yourself how far it has been shaped by the audit
findings.

The Secular Society

By now you may be thinking 'that's all very well,
but what has any of it to do with me?'. I realise
that the detailed findings will be of little interest
to most readers – that is why I have omitted most
of the detail! But it shows the types of information
an audit of this kind provides. Any church would
find that this kind of knowledge about their area
and its people, and about their own membership,
provided a sharper focus to their mission as well
as a greater awareness of their own weaknesses.
These two factors taken together can only have a
salutary effect in driving us back to planning and
prayer. It may be true that those churches whose
congregation is drawn wholly or mainly from the
local community have less need of such an audit
and would be in for fewer surprises. However to

those churches – and there are a good number of them, especially in towns – where there is a large divergence between the make-up of the congregation and the people of the local community, I would say 'Can you afford *not* to do an audit?'

Any business with a product to sell needs to do some basic market research before it can adopt an effective sales strategy. While there are dangers in pressing too hard the analogy between the Church and a commercial venture, the good sense of this in general terms is apparent. The 'product' must match the 'market' to some extent. There are many worrying signs that for too long the Church has been content to answer questions people are no longer asking.

Many church people's thinking still seems to be based on an underlying, if unspoken, assumption that Britain is basically a 'Christian country'. The facts no longer support such an assumption. Examine how far the Christian faith underlies crucial areas of our society – standards of conduct in private and public life and in business; the aims set before us by political and other leaders; the preoccupations of the media; the content of our education curriculum; ordinary people's personal priorities and values, or simply the extent to which they even know what the Christian gospel is – as distinct from having views about the Church as an institution. We can hardly escape the conclusion that the secularisation of society in 1990s Britain is almost complete. George Carey has described secularisation as 'a process of change within society, either deliberate or unconscious, which leaves God out, electing for the material in preference to the spiritual, the worldly over against eternal values'.[4] He adds that this process is complete when faith 'becomes private and optional'.

This seems to me to describe the present situation exactly. Those who pull the levers in society are concerned, even if with the best of motives, only with the things of this world. Their decisions are based on the premise that there are no other considerations. The powerful effect of the media ensures that the great majority of people think the same way. They think like this not as a result of careful consideration leading to a rational conclusion, but simply as an assumption which need not be stated and should not be questioned. People say, 'If you need religion, and find it helps you, that's fine ... just so long as you don't try and force your beliefs onto me.' This kind of magnanimous toleration is the most that we can expect: the idea that, if the Christian gospel is true, then it *must* affect society, is considered outrageous. That is why the very publication of *Faith in the City* in 1985 caused such discomfiture amongst politicians and aroused the old cry 'the Church should keep its nose out of politics'. The institutional Church has to some extent been complicit in this process of secularisation – as have we individual members – if only by our silence. If the Decade of Evangelism is to make any impact on our nation, Christians need to be fully alive to this situation. We must spare no effort to see that we are addressing people where they really are, not where we imagine them to be or, worse still, think they ought to be. Against such a background an audit of the 'patch' for which we are responsible can play a vital part. Who is really out there? What do they do? What do they want?

What do they think about us? If they do not come near us, why not . . . ?

You Too Can Have An Audit!

It does not require a great deal of expertise to mount this kind of audit. Help is available from a number of quarters.[5] But one or two words of warning are necessary. It involves much hard work. This means that, although an audit should never become an end in itself, *for a time* it will need to be given high priority. The people directly involved must be thoroughly convinced of its value. Everyone concerned must accept from the outset that the point lies ultimately not in the assembling of facts for their own sake, but in a plan for action to which the membership – not just the leadership – will be committed.

Lastly, let me pass on a tip. When we were finding it very difficult to get the idea off the ground we discovered, by a chance comment, that the name was putting some people off. For some the word 'audit' has heavy financial implications – with overtones of snooping around to catch somebody out! Against this background 'parish audit' apparently had a somewhat threatening ring. Most people seemed far more comfortable with 'parish review'. Another name sometimes used is 'mission audit' – although this still contains the dreaded A-word, it does identify far more clearly the ultimate objective, as well as using a word to which the average person in the pew may relate more easily.

A postscript. As well as a great deal of hard

work, you will get a certain amount of fun out of
it! Here are some one-liners from our own visits.

Q. Do you practise a religion?
A.   No, but I am Church of England.
A.   I believe in God, but I don't have time.
A.   My wife's a Christian, but I'm more a beer
     and skittles man myself.

Q. What do you like about Boscombe?
A.   You can pick your own fruit in the green-
     grocers.

**Q. What social problems are there in
     Boscombe?**
A.   I don't get involved.   (Quite so!)

And, just occasionally you will be brought up very
short – as when someone said 'Not many people go
to St John's do they? If they do, they're not locals'.
A statement of the obvious, certainly . . . but it was
someone with no church connections whatsoever
who had put her finger right on the sore spot.

CHAPTER SIX
ALL CHANGE

All this served to confirm what we had already begun to realise. Throughout 1988 we were confronted with the need to turn outwards to the people of the locality. There were, Godfrey told us, hundreds with poor mental health; drug and alcohol addiction; difficulty in relating to others because of past traumas, often in childhood; involvement in the occult; appalling loneliness; living conditions which depressed and degraded them; in some cases no living accommodation at all. The list seemed endless. But what had it to do with us? These people did not impinge on us. As we came to church in our cars most of us hardly even noticed the vagrants and alcoholics who frequented the gardens across the road. If they strayed on to the seats outside the church, we just ignored them.

But that was precisely the point. Could we go on ignoring them? How could we square our belief in the gospel with a highly selective approach to its application? Our numbers were growing. We were glad when people joined us from other churches, especially if they were potential leaders. We rejoiced even more over converts who grew into bright, articulate Christians. 'Nice people make

nice Christians,' we used to joke. They fitted in
with the image we had of ourselves as a church
– later confirmed by our audit – comfortable,
property-owning, car-driving, mostly either under
30 or over 45, and (as far as anyone could tell)
respectable.

Of course, none of these characteristics is repre-
hensible. A problem arises only if they distance us
from people who do not share them. Granted that
the new St John's Centre had started to provide
a point of real contact with local people and their
needs, the church family as a whole was still
a largely inward-looking community – not consciously trying to be exclusive, just busy with our
own worthy preoccupations. Many gifts were being
discovered, especially in teaching and leading the
young. Organisations were generally flourishing.
Worship was being enriched by additions to the
preaching team and widening musical horizons.
Support for overseas mission was being maintained. God's blessing was in evidence in individual lives. But, if we are honest, most of us never
gave more than a fleeting thought to the people on
the streets outside. They went their way; we went
ours. They were 'the world'; we were 'the Church'.

We sometimes sing:

> May his Spirit fill our praise,
> Guide our thoughts and change our ways;
> God in Christ has come to stay,
> We can see his power today.[1]

But the truth is that most people do not really
like change. There are, of course, a few who
thrive on it – we happen to be blessed with one

as our Vicar! But the British temperament generally feels threatened, rather than excited, by the
prospect of change. Historically that has produced
a stable, rather than revolutionary, society, a benefit offset by a reluctance to change when change
is needed. The disadvantages of this in industry
and commerce are all too obvious today. Nowhere
is ambivalence towards change more apparent
than in the topsy-turvy world of party politics.
Notwithstanding that the Opposition's role is to
show that the Government's policies are wrong
and should be changed, the slightest hint of a
policy change is greeted with derision as a sign of
vacillation and weakness. It was this phenomenon
which gave rise to the 1980s' most quoted pun,
when Margaret Thatcher rebutted a charge of
making what her critics described as a U-turn by
the now-famous misquotation of Christopher Fry:
'You turn if you like – the lady's not for turning.'

Instinctively people feel that a dogged determination not to be blown off course, come what may,
is a cardinal virtue. In many ways it is indeed
admirable. But it has its dangers. In commerce
inflexibility leads to lost opportunities. In politics
determination not to change course can stand in
the way of progress. And in a spiritual context a
dogged, head down, 'I know what I believe' type
of Christianity can fail to discern the signs of the
times and prevent us from being alert to new ways
in which the Spirit of God may be prompting us.

A Pilgrim Church

Throughout the Bible the people of God are
depicted as a *pilgrim* people. Ever since God

called Abram to leave his native country and go
'to a land I will show you' (Genesis 12:1), God's
people have been on the move. There is a dynamic
quality about them . . . going where he calls, being
drawn towards him in repentance and sent out
in mission. Indeed, Scripture attributes an essentially temporary quality to the whole of life. This
applies to 'secular' things – for example Jesus tells
us to 'store up treasure in heaven' rather than on
earth (Matthew 6:19–21), and St Paul exhorts us
to set our minds on things above rather than on
earthly things (Colossians 3:1–4). But God's Word
insists that even 'spiritual' things, despite being
our link with things 'beyond the veil', should also
be seen as transitory and incomplete here. So St
Paul describes spiritual gifts as imperfect and
passing away (1 Corinthians 13:8–12); and the
writer to the Hebrews issues his telling reminder
that 'here we have no continuing city' (Hebrews
13:14 AV).

This pilgrim, transitory, incomplete existence
implies a frame of mind diametrically opposite
to the conservation ethos which currently per-
vades life in Britain. One is dynamic, the other
static; one seeks to make things new, the other
to preserve the old; one looks eagerly forward, the
other conscientiously backward; one tends to see
change in terms of opportunity and growth, the
other in terms of threat and decay. I must tread
carefully! I am not encouraging a thoughtless
abandonment of the past, or defending change for
its own sake: both attitudes are common amongst
'progressives', within the Church as elsewhere.
There is a counterfeit of the true pilgrim spirit
which is merely the restlessness of insecurity.

Nevertheless, if the Church is to be true to the
scriptural image of God's people, it should exhibit
a general *tendency* towards moving on, travelling
light, letting go of its past willingly when called to
do so. I realise that for some this assertion will
automatically discredit anything else I have to
say. I must accept that risk. What is quite unacceptable is that the conservation mentality has
become so politically correct as to be beyond questioning – so that anybody doing so is likely to be
branded ignorant, irresponsible, or probably both!

Facing up to the need for change on a number
of fronts is a major challenge for the Church as an
institution in our day. Will it:

- look forward in faith, or backward in
  nostalgia?
- recognise that God is still actively leading
  us into new understanding of the truth and
  new sacrifices, opportunities and adven-
  tures; or regard its chief responsibility
  as clinging tenaciously to things received
  from the past?

The Church's response is critical to its mission.
Behaving as if the Holy Spirit ceased his creative
work at some point (arbitrary, but always well in
the past!) means the Decade of Evangelism will fail
to make the impact on the nation for which many
long and pray. Some of these broader issues will be
touched on in a later chapter; but here I identify
some of the areas where we in St John's were most
in need of change, and see how it is starting to come
about. It will, after all, be in the local context that

readers will have to work out their own attitudes, and face their own challenges, to change.

Changing Our Priorities

Although the 'phases' of this process were not perceptible at the time, hindsight enables them to be seen analytically. First God was calling us to change the focus of our priorities. For a church majoring on 'sound teaching' this involves some searching questions. A hallmark of the evangelical tradition has always been its emphasis on God's truth, revealed in the written word of Scripture and the incarnate Word, Jesus Christ. Many have given their lives contending for the truth. Even those Christians who do not easily identify with evangelical insights would regard such single-minded zeal as a noble thing. But dangers lurk even here.

It is all too easy to confuse the unchanging nature of God's truth with an unchanging presentation of it. Most of us have heard the gospel presented in the street using language or techniques belonging to a bygone age. Such dated expression makes it less, not more, likely that the truth will actually be heard above the 'cringe factor'. This applies equally to building up God's people through worship and teaching. Priority must be given to intelligibility. The Church is charged to preserve the deposit of truth itself, not any particular means of expressing it. The purpose of that charge is that truth may be *communicated* in the Church and to the world, not *enshrined* for

our own appreciation in a specific idiom. Despite
the protestations of the traditionalists, this does
not always come down to a stark choice between
intelligibility and beauty. Certainly it will involve
some sacrifice of personal taste and inclination:
what a sad irony that our common life in the
Church is often the last place where we expect
to have to apply the sacrificial principle of 'dying
to self' which lies at the heart of discipleship.

A second danger is less easily recognised. Many
Christians see 'truth' in propositional form. For
them it is encapsulated in a series of doctrinal
statements or propositions, derived from close
study of the Scriptures or the traditions of the
Church. To absorb all these propositions is to
'know the truth'. The more I reflect on this
approach, the more dissatisfied with it I become
– for two reasons. First it diminishes the splendour
of God's truth by limiting it to the measure of the
human mind. Secondly it is what I would call 'non-
incarnational': it makes it easy to divorce what we
believe from how we *live*, in particular how we
relate to others. Belief and action are kept in separate compartments. Rather than risk exposing our
beliefs to be tempered in the heat of everyday trials
and relationships, we concentrate on keeping the
propositions intact, using them primarily as a code
by which to test the 'soundness' of others.

I should be amongst the last to minimise the
importance of contending for the truth. In our
liberal and multi-faith society it is more important
than ever that Christians affirm boldly and without compromise the simple, unique and eternal
truth of the revealed gospel of Christ. Nevertheless, if we regard our relationships with others as

primarily a crusade for the truth, then we are
eccentric Christians. This simply means off-centre!
To suppose that discipleship is a matter of believing the right things, and trying to get others to
see them in the same way, is a travesty of the
New Testament. There those adjudged 'good' or
'profitable' in God's kingdom have sought above
all to respond to the call to *servanthood*. (See e.g.
Matthew 25:14–30.) We should put that first, and
seek constantly to develop our understanding of
the truth against that background. Then, because
our beliefs will have been tested and, where necessary, shaped by practical service, we shall be
wiser – though probably not so comfortable – in
our believing.

Do we allow ourselves to understand Christian
truth from Christian living in this way? God leads
his children through life's varied experiences, not
least those which cause us pain, precisely in order
that we grow in our understanding of him and his
ways – that is, of truth. (See Psalm 119:71; James
1:2–4; 2 Peter 3:18.) Or are we doggedly intent on
believing exactly the same things in the same way
throughout our life? If we apprehend God's truth
today in all respects in exactly the same way as
we did years ago, we should ask ourselves some
serious questions about our growth.

At St John's some had fallen into that danger.
In November 1988, Godfrey Taylor wrote to the
church family:

Over the years, Bible teaching has always
been high on the agenda at St John's – and
you can rest assured that it always will be.
But the New Testament says some stern

things about hearing the word without doing
it . . . True discipleship will always, sooner or
later, mean action – action that is costly in
terms of time, effort and maybe self-respect.
Now is the right time for us to take a close
look at how God is calling us to use our
buildings and the talents of our members
to respond to the needs and concerns of our
parish.

We really did not know what those needs and
concerns were. Concentrating hard on God's truth,
we had largely failed to notice the crying need all
around us for God's love to be seen in action. To
see how God has begun to deal with this we take
up the story where we left it in Chapter Four.

When the Centre opened in 1985, Godfrey was
already thinking about the next project. Some
years earlier a picture of St John's with the
words 'The Church of the Open Door' had come
to him. Now God began to show a number of
us that it was not enough simply to study the
truth and teach it to like-minded people from
the surrounding area. We were also required to
show his love in service, in particular to those on
our doorstep who, although far from like-minded,
were among those for whom God had entrusted us
with his gospel. Or, as the Bishop had said in 1981,
we had 'a responsibility for embodying the love of
God for every person in the whole neighbourhood
– no one left out'.

But how were we to respond to this new impera-
tive? At one time the answer would probably have
been to organise a parish mission. Nothing wrong
with that: but in fact God appeared to be asking

us to do something quite different. There was a growing sense that his hand was now on the tiller, changing our course in spite of ourselves. The immediate action demanded of us was not just to go on *declaring his truth* but to start in a new way *demonstrating his love*. This would be much more long-term, and ultimately far more costly, than a special mission. The phrase that kept appearing in sermons and prayer meetings was 'availability-evangelism'. The first stage was to say to the people of the area, 'We are here and in Christ's name we care about you.'

Changing our Building

But our doors were bolted and barred for six and a half days a week! The signal given out to the neighbourhood was 'We're *not* here and we *don't* care about you.' To be available we had to be open: on the visible level that meant literally opening the church doors. But for what? Much as we loved it as our place of worship, there was little about the church building which would enable us to serve people coming in off the streets seeking help, advice or friendship. If we were right in identifying God's call to change the focus of our priorities – and we felt increasingly sure that we were – it seemed he was now calling us to consider changing our *buildings*. The one seemed to lead inevitably to the other. We needed to re-apply the lesson of the Centre project – 'seeing people through buildings'.

Naturally, there were many months of discussions in PCC; a committee was formed to develop

the basic concept; and the church was called to
special meetings to pray and seek God's will
together. Sufficient unanimity emerged to justify
commissioning an architect to prepare an outline
scheme to turn the west end of the church into
an area which would provide separate accommodation for visitors during the week, but could be
taken into the main worship area when necessary to accommodate large congregations. We
also needed (a) quiet room(s) where people could
talk privately, coffee-bar facilities and toilets. The
design challenge given to Maurice Taylor, a very
experienced London-based architect, was considerable – to meet the operational requirements of
the weekday ministry we envisaged, at the same
time enhancing facilities for worship ... and
all this without detriment to a beautiful Gothic
interior.

Those who understand architects' plans spent
the early summer of 1988 poring over them: the
rest of us looked at his drawings and an impressive scale model! He had risen magnificently to
the challenge. The old building, a long, narrow
tube used for only three or four hours a week
because it was suitable for very little else, could be
transformed into a place of such flexibility that it
could be used for a wide variety of purposes for as
many hours as we could staff it. The potential was
very exciting. The estimated cost of the scheme,
including new sound and lighting systems for
the whole building, was £210,000. Would the
church family, which appeared to have caught
the vision of what might be done, dig deep into
their pockets again for the second time in five
years?

A Pledge Sunday was set aside in July for members to indicate the financial support they hoped to be able to give. It was an unforgettable day. The whole church family gathered for all-age worship in an air of almost tangible expectancy. As soon as the service began, a totally spontaneous atmosphere of joyful confidence took us over. There was a barely-controlled excitement about what was going to happen. When the moment came for us to make our pledges, everyone marched or shuffled around the church in an enormous, untidy, singing procession, putting their pledge into a large almsdish. This symbolised in a powerful way that, as a church, we were on the move. There was an overriding sense of unity of purpose. When it came to the end of the day we all felt that we were waiting to hear not what we had achieved, but what God had done. He had given us, in that one day, over £185,000. There was a great Doxology! Subsequently the total cost rose to over £250,000, but by January 1989 promises had risen to £200,000. The local charitable trust which had helped to finance St John's Centre again made a generous donation, and further interest-free loans eased cash-flow problems while gifts from members covenanted over four years were actually received. A few weeks before the project opened the total cost had been covered by gifts and promises.

Events moved swiftly. The necessary planning permissions were obtained from ecclesiastical and local authorities, tenders were sought and a local firm was awarded the contract. Christmas 1988 was notable for a sense of impending disorder. When the youngsters from the Bournemouth

Music Centre crowded the church for their Christmas concert in early December, several rows of pews had already been unscrewed from the floor ready for removal. I suppose the result of such instability was inevitable: fortunately nobody was hurt! The following week the builders moved in, and soon there was chaos. A solid wooden screen was erected (and promptly decorated for Christmas!) two-thirds of the way down the nave, shutting off the building site from the worship area. Now even the most unobservant church members, those who had allowed all the planning, the excitement and the chance to contribute, to pass them by, could not escape the fact that something was happening. As pneumatic drills went to work, the whole building always seemed to be covered in dust, however hard the verger and an army of helpers worked to clean it. Even I noticed this ... I had to wipe the dust off the organ keys before each service. On occasions we had to huddle together to get everyone in – things were getting serious!

Those first six months of 1989 were a time of chaos, bustle and excitement – and growing apprehension. What had we started? Where would it lead? What should we be able to offer the people who came in? This last question became sharper when the audit results confirmed in graphic detail the needs and problems of our parishioners. We felt inadequate. We were just the same people as we had always been ... a group of individual believers with little or no experience in dealing with the kind of people we were about to encounter. I deliberately use the word 'individual', because that is basically what we were.

Of course there were close relationships and deep
friendships within the congregation. But overall
a sturdy individualism still characterised many
of our activities. This is one of the less positive
characteristics of traditional evangelical churches
majoring on 'sound teaching'. Hearing sermons
can be – often is – a solo activity. In itself it does
nothing to break down the 'my faith is a private
matter' attitude often vaunted as the essence of
scriptural spirituality, but for which, in fact, we
search the New Testament in vain. As a sense
of corporate responsibility for those outside the
church had been lacking among us, so too had that
strong sense of being 'members of one another'
which may often be observed in churches whose
life has been touched by the renewing power of
the Spirit.

God had called us to change our *focus*; we were
already in the process of changing our *buildings*;
now we *ourselves* needed to be changed – from
a group of dedicated individuals into a dedicated
fellowship with a common purpose and a corporate
dynamic.

Changing People

It was here that John Richards played a crucial
part. A former St John's choirboy, he now offers a
ministry to churches under the banner 'Renewal
Servicing'. Shortly before the West End opened
he met with the 40 or so people who had offered,
with varying degrees of diffidence, to join the rota
for duty in the Church of the Open Door. The title
of his session – *'The Transformed Community'*

– could hardly have been more appropriate. Looking back now on what he had to say, it was a truly prophetic ministry. Not only did he see with uncanny accuracy some of the things we were subsequently to experience; he also put his finger on aspects of our life that needed dealing with. He emphasised that in becoming the Church of the Open Door we were embarking on what amounted to a complete U-turn. He warned that the change would take a lot of working through. Whereas we had been used to coming into the church building 'to meet God and other Christians', it would now become a place where we should encounter spiritualists, occultists, agnostics and atheists who 'will not be wearing Scripture Union badges or clutching well-worn Bibles'. How right he was – we have had them all, and more!

We should need a U-turn not only in how we viewed the church building, but in our concepts of the gospel. Although *we* knew that the people we met were sinners needing the salvation that Jesus alone can bring, we should not expect that to be *their* starting point. If we tried to start there, they might experience their visit to us 'not as an Open Door but as one slammed in their face'. Our idea of the gospel had been too small. Of course it was about the good news of sins forgiven – but it was about more than that. Christ has the answer to every aspect of the human condition – loneliness, disintegration, meaninglessness, insecurity, pain, bereavement, inferiority, resentment, anger, alienation, guilt. We could learn by observing how he went about his earthly ministry: the first contact with people

must be at their point of need. To find this out
we should have to listen, not talk. And then –
a crucial comment – *'Unless we are as open as
our doors are, this place may still be a place of
rejection.'*

The benefit of hindsight shows the wisdom of
many other things he said. For instance, that
the promise of Christ's presence 'where two or
three are gathered together' in his name (Matthew
18:20 AV) applies not only to gathering for worship, but where we meet to help, love, care and
support others in his name. We should try to be
specifically conscious of the presence of the risen
Christ as we seek to minister to people in the West
End. As a fellowship we must look to our own spiritual nourishment and wellbeing, because 'visitors to the open Door will only encounter *what we
have*'. He ended by reinforcing emphatically in the
context of the Open Door the importance of learning what it means to be members of one another:

My own impression in caring and counselling
is that the Protestant respect for the individual conscience means that people tend to
'shop around' for the ministry that they find
most congenial – which is likely to be the one
that is least demanding!

Do we need some sort of structure or frame-
work . . . which expresses our common sub-
mission to Jesus and his Spirit? Are we a
gathering of individuals all of whom have
a hot line to Jesus (and that is very important), or are we willing to forego a little of
that in order that Jesus' hot line may be to
the fellowship as a whole? The Open Door

> venture suggests to me that you are already
> well on the way into corporate hearing and
> corporate obedience. That's good. Protestant-
> ism is the most fragmented branch of the
> Church precisely because of its respect for
> the individual.

He may have thought we were further on than in
fact we were! Certainly he foresaw the lessons we
were to learn as the venture developed. We still
have much to learn, but an increasing number of
us are at least now aware that these things are on
God's agenda for us.

1989 could be summed up in the phrase 'all
change'. Not quite all, of course. In any church
there are some who remain detached from what
is occupying the attention of the rest; and in a
church of several hundred members there were
bound to be a number who remained unaffected
by, even largely unaware of, all that was going on.
But going on it was.

We were soon to discover that the church building was no less a place of *worship* for becoming
also a place of *work*, sometimes hard, dirty, unre-
warding work: indeed, there is a feeling that the
whole building has been hallowed afresh by the
new work that goes on in it in Christ's name.
Similarly, we were no less the *worshipping community* for the fact that many of us now spent
time as *working partners*. In fact, we have found
our worship enriched and deepened because many
of those worshipping together on a Sunday have
worked together in the previous week. As the
visible changes took place in the church building,
other, more far-reaching changes needed to take

place – were starting to take place – in us as 'the church'. In a way we did not realise at the time, one was symbolic of the other.

St John's had been a lively centre for the proclamation of God's love in Boscombe for almost a hundred years. Now, as God called us to embark on a new phase in that task, he had challenged us to a new, enlarged focus on our priorities and wonderfully provided us with the resources to adapt our premises. Here is a principle of discipleship: God calls – we obey – God provides. Now the Holy Spirit was beginning to enlarge our vision, our love and our capacity for caring. Now we could sing 'guide our thoughts and change our ways' with rather more conviction! But, before we threw the doors wide open, there was something else we needed to learn. It was intensely practical. You might think it too obvious even to mention. Although the people who were about to start coming through those doors would have many different problems, they would almost all have one common need – someone to listen to them. Perhaps you are a good listener? No? Nor am I! Urgent action was needed.

CHAPTER SEVEN
LEARNING TO LISTEN

I ought not to suggest that eavesdropping is the same thing as listening! But I must admit that one of the few enjoyable things about the otherwise exhausting and wasteful time I spent on rush-hour trains during 23 years as a commuter was the opportunities it afforded for people-watching. Cooped up for a couple of hours every day with a varying selection of fellow human beings there was always plenty to observe – and to listen to. Then, when I reached London, there was the District Line, and the office cleaners going home presumably to breakfast and bed.

* * *

"E 'ardly knows where 'e is wiv the pain sometimes.' 'Oo, I know. It's jest the same wiv my Arfur's leg. Course, 'e's bin like it since the war . . .'

'Wakes up in the night wiv it, sometimes . . . gets this sort of bruised feeling round 'is 'eart, 'e does. On'y the uvver day I says to 'im "Bert," I says, "know what I fink? I fink you oughter . . ."'

'A lot of the boys as was in Burma 'as the same trouble wiv their legs, but that don't . . .'

''E's under the doctor wiv it, but yer know them doctors . . . sez it was jes' indergestion, an' 'e 'ad the nerve to say as 'ow if 'e was to drink a bit less . . . I ask yer!'

'Course, Arfur fought 'e might 'ave ter 'ave it taken right off one time, y'know, like 'is sister Daisy's cousin . . .'

'I mean, 'e never comes 'ome not what you'd call . . . y'know . . . not reely . . .'

* * *

The train rattled into Mansion House station and I got out, leaving Dolly and Flo to finish their 'really nice talk' about their respective husbands' problems. Drop in at a suburban cocktail party and you might hear the same kind of conversation. The accents would be different, of course, and probably the subject matter. But the common feature would be two participants giving out a great deal and taking in very little, their brains 90 per cent on transmit and only 10 per cent on receive. That 10 per cent just about enables them to stay within the same broad subject area – the garden, the Conservative Party, their husbands' shortcomings or their wives' habit of spending money like water – but that level of awareness serves only to trigger a further input from each participant of something he or she wants to say. There is no real meeting of minds, no listening and responding.

Does it matter? In most cases not very much – certainly in the kind of chatter that goes on in buses, at parties, over the lunch table or in the office. But in some circumstances it matters intensely. How many people have resorted to desperate measures because they needed to talk and could not find anybody to listen? It was the realisation of this which led to the establishment of the Samaritans.

The Need to Listen

From the time we first began to think seriously about the Church of the Open Door we had always envisaged that people would want to come in for a chat. Being in one of Britain's premier holiday resorts, we were already used to large numbers of visitors, and obviously we all chatted with them after the service ... well, some of us did, anyway. So if the church was to be open daily, all we needed was to make sure we had enough people to be there to chat with them. But in the months leading up to the opening of the project the Holy Spirit prompted us to think more deeply. It was not going to be enough to chat inconsequentially about where people came from and how they were enjoying their holiday. Some would want to talk on a more serious level. Following our audit, we realised local people would come in looking for help ... maybe with spiritual problems. Well ... we could always ring the Vicar and ask him to come and talk to them!

That was not the answer, and we knew it. This was not just about opening the building: it was about opening up 'the church', i.e. ourselves as God's people. In making the vision of the Open Door into a reality, we had already (somewhat to our own surprise!) surmounted one major challenge in meeting the cost of the building work.

Now, as we saw that work nearing completion, we faced our next major hurdle. It was going to involve an even greater leap of faith. We needed people – a great many people – willing to give *themselves*, day in day out, not just to be present in the church building, but ready to listen. Really listen! Not only to the words people were using, but to what they were actually saying . . . and the two things can be very different.

A Forgotten Skill

Most of us are not good at listening . . . probably not as good as our forbears. Television has conditioned us to having an endless stream of information pouring out at us while we eat, knit, talk among ourselves or (if surveys are to be believed) make love. Unless something of exceptional interest comes on, we do not expect to give the information source much attention. Research has shown that people retain a great deal more of what they see than of what they hear. This discovery has changed, for example, educational techniques away from the classroom lecture to more visual means of presentation, and where possible to 'hands-on' experience.

All this has produced a fundamental shift in the way people relate to each other. Indeed, rapid technological advances in everyday things – automatic cash dispensers, fax machines, shopping/banking by phone, computer games – seem to be ushering in a culture where people will not have to relate to each other at all. I believe the

long-term effects of this will have a significant,
possibly devastating, impact on human society.
Already many of us do not *expect* ever to have
to sit and listen to another person, and many are
not *willing* to do so. How long before we are simply
not *able* to do so?

Unfortunately, this affects Christians as much
as anybody else – hence the the ten-minute
sermon rule in many places! In our informal
exchanges how often we say 'How are you?',
but then do not listen to the reply carefully
enough to discern that behind the words there
may be a cry for attention or help. When this
has happened to a needy person a few times,
they stop even trying to communicate their need,
and reply 'Me? Oh . . . I'm OK thanks.' Why do
we tend, even within the fellowship of believers,
to be so superficial in our relationships? Giving
ourselves the benefit of the doubt, let us say
it is probably because we just do not think. At
other times, though, is it not because we *do*
think? We think just deeply enough to know
that, if we really listen, we may have to get
involved.

We MUST Learn to Listen

So what of St Paul's injunction to 'carry each
other's burdens'? He presented this not as an
optional extra of Christian neighbourliness, but
as a basic of discipleship, the way in which we
'fulfil the law of Christ' (Galatians 6:2). This does
indeed match up with one of the few instances

where Christ himself explicitly lays down the law. He says: 'A new *command* I give you: Love one another' ... and in case we miss the point, he continues: 'As I have loved you, so you must love one another' (John 13:34). What Jesus asks of us, he has already demonstrated. How often, although he himself was tired, and probably preoccupied with what lay ahead, he stopped and listened to someone so that he could meet their need. In this area we have both his command and his example. We are to get involved with people, and must be ready for that involvement to be costly and sacrificial. And real involvement will almost always start with real listening.

Becoming a listening fellowship was not going to be just a question of willingness, but also of know-how. Listening, like everything else worthwhile, involves technique. How could we teach and learn that technique? Obviously we could not turn dozens of people into fully-trained counsellors, although it did help that one or two folk had already been trained in contexts such as the Samaritans, Life, and Rape Crisis Line. We needed a way of providing people with a basic awareness of the skills involved, and the chance to practise them in a friendly, no-risk environment before unleashing them on our unsuspecting visitors!

The 'Listening' Course

We found a Christian Caring course produced by the Scripture Union. It is designed to help 'ordinary Christians' who

- want to be better listeners;
- want to be more effective in developing relationships with others;
- find they are the sort of person to whom other people turn for help or advice on personal issues.

It aims to teach participants to listen attentively, be seen to listen and give feedback to show they have received what people are saying and feeling; to understand and practise empathy; to become aware of the significance of body language; to help others to 'open up' about their problems and confront rather than evade them. Groups of ten or twelve people met once a week, sometimes with assignments between sessions. (By the end of the week in which my wife's homework was to observe the body language of those around her I was afraid to twitch a muscle!) They were trying to learn to listen so that it is obvious that they are doing so. Even professionals such as doctors or clergy, for whom good listening skills might be regarded as a basic skill, often seem to transmit rather than receive. Maybe they *are* listening: if so, they do not let it show! How much more, then, does the 'amateur' need help here.

Godfrey Taylor led a pilot course in spring 1989. But we should need many more people than that to staff the Open Door project for six days a week. Running more ten-week courses would absorb more time and energy than he could possibly spare. In any case, God was developing our understanding that in Christ's Body the needs of his work can be met by the gifts he has given to his people. For practical reasons, and to be true to the vision of every-member ministry, we sought someone to undertake this key training role.

It needed someone special. Fortunately we had them. Rhys and Gwenda Lewis, a married couple in their late fifties, would not think of themselves as 'special' at all – rather the opposite. Rhys had spent all his adult working life in shoes . . . selling them, that is! He came from Welsh stock, though he was brought up in London. Gwenda's forbears also came from Wales, where her grandfather had been a Congregational minister. She had worked in nursery education, but devoted the main years of her life to raising their family of four children. She already had experience of counselling in the Life organisation.

But let me not make the common mistake of pigeon-holing people by their work or family origin. It is true that to some extent we all are what we inherit; but it is also true that God makes us all 'one-off' originals right from the start. And then we become what all our experiences make us into. That is why God leads us through all kinds of things in our lives. Often it is the 'bad' things (from our earthbound perspective) which, eventually, mark the stamp of servanthood on us. This is a helpful way of understanding the promise (Romans 8:28–29) that all things are working for our good. The promise is to those who are 'called according to his purpose', defined as our being 'conformed to the likeness of his Son', who came to serve in complete obedience to his Father even though that entailed suffering and ultimately death (Philippians 2:5–8). From a truly Christian perspective a person's age or occupation are irrelevant: it is what they have allowed God to make of them, how far they are becoming conformed to the likeness of Jesus, which truly defines what they *are*. I make this small digression to emphasise why no Christian can ever properly be described as 'ordinary', because God has reached out and touched their individual lives and is making of them something which to him, even if we cannot see it, is unique and special.

Rhys and Gwenda both made a personal commitment to Christ many years ago. But things have not always been easy: they have both known hardship and trauma in their own lives and in their family, and at times the flame of faith has burnt low. They have emerged with a Christian maturity which goes deep, and both of them have a gift for sharing their faith with others in a natural way. At the time in question Rhys was a churchwarden and Gwenda had been occasionally involved in various forms of informal pastoral ministry within the church. It seemed right to ask them, with their proven track record, and equipped as they were with the natural abilities and spiritual gifts needed, to take on this vital role of training those who would be crucial to the success of the Open Door ministry. But they were not at all sure they were the right people for the job. They felt inadequate. They did not feel immediately drawn to it. Looking back, they would say they were put under some human pressure to accept it. Looking at the results that have flowed from their decision to take it on, others would say they were responding to the prompting of the Holy Spirit.

Rhys and Gwenda typify what is needed if a church is to move purposefully in the direction God calls. A church can only do that if individual members set themselves to do it, maybe against their own inclinations. I always feel sad when I hear individual Christians talk about their own church as 'they' (usually in a negative context): in this thought mode, 'they' are the people who do things . . . 'I' am the person to whom things are done. When more of us start to realise that 'they' are nothing more nor less than the sum total of all the 'I's, then 'the church' will be on the move.

Rhys and Gwenda played a key role for over three years in training those in the front line of our new encounter with the world beyond our doors. But I have also singled them out for special mention because they typify numbers of folk at St John's who have brought their gifts and put them at God's disposal. Mostly they would think of themselves as 'ordinary', not gifted at all. And yet one of the most important – and humbling – lessons we have learnt is that when such people simply make themselves available to God, he can make extraordinary use of them. And it is only because they have made this offering of themselves that anything has happened at all. The vision for the Church of the Open Door may have come via the leadership, but it could never have become a reality without the response of many individual Christians. They were not so much responding to a call from the leadership, but to the prompting of the Holy Spirit. What we are witnessing is true spiritual renewal. Renewal has tended to present itself in more spectacular clothing. This is the practical manifestation of renewal ... renewal with dirty hands. We are being *renewed for service*.

What The Course Has Taught Us

Well over a hundred people have now been given what Gwenda has described as this 'introductory toolbag' for work in the West End. In age, background and disposition they were a rich mixture. Some found role-play exercises totally alien, never really grasping what was going on. The leaders took others on the course with real doubts about their ability to cope, only to be gloriously surprised. One quite elderly man appeared completely bemused by the course, but during it he prayed aloud for the first time in his life – and has not stopped since! Many participants have said that they learnt things about themselves during the sessions which have spilled over into their daily lives. A headmistress who expected just to brush up her skills found herself re-thinking her attitudes towards parents and staff. Someone else reported improved communication with their own teenage children.

Designed simply to prepare individuals to work in the Open Door project, the listening course has had a more far-reaching effect on the church ... and who knows where else? Most of the Spirit's activity goes on below the surface of people's lives. But something is discernible, though difficult to define. Almost a quarter of our total adult membership have now been through this course together. Members of each group have been encouraged to pray with and for one another, and

to seek to share and solve their own problems
together. It has been very moving for the leaders to
see new supportive relationships forming between
people who previously knew one another, if at all,
only superficially.

Learning to care for one another in a new way
has been an unexpected by-product of meeting
to learn to listen to others. It has all sprung
from the simple fact that many have now learnt,
in Gwenda's words, that 'listening is far more
than just sitting and nodding the head ... *active
listening* involves an awareness not only of what
the other person is saying, but of what they are
doing, thinking and feeling ...'.

Every Christian A Listener?

This prompts some questions. Have you learnt to
listen? Do you hold back because of where it might
lead or what it might cost? If you are a church
leader, can you glimpse the effect it might have
if your congregation learnt to listen like this?
They would probably be less docile – but should
that worry you? These are vital questions. Our
experience has uncovered something most of us
might not have stumbled across in a lifetime's
churchgoing – that much of the shallowness in
church fellowships stems from failure to listen.
Burden-sharing is not optional, but the way to
'fulfil the law of Christ'. We all need to take it
seriously. Of course, this does not mean we shall
all be called to take part in something like the
Open Door project. That is not the point. But we
do all know people who need help with carrying

a burden. Do we really understand what that
burden is? What about that chap who seems a
bit strange; that woman who reacts in a way we
do not understand; that person who always seems
unnecessarily prickly? Have we tried to find out
why? Do we care?

People simply do not listen to one another.
This may be unconscious, or deliberate. It may
be because they do not make time, or because
they do not know how. Whatever the reason,
it represents a vacuum at the centre of church
life. Our experience shows that it is worth doing
something about it. It helps us become more obedi-
ent and effective disciples of the compassionate
Lord Jesus. But it is also as we *listen* that our
sense of belonging to one another grows, and we
begin to discover much more of the joy and vitality,
as well as sharing the pain and heartache, which
should flow from being 'members together of the
Body of Christ'.

CHAPTER EIGHT
WESTENDERS

Sunday, 11 June 1989. At last the talking, planning, noise and disruption were over. The builders' dust had settled, and everything was resplendent and in order. As the evening sun shone through the west window, touching the new woodwork with a golden glow, we knew that God had enabled us to make not just a tool for his work, but a thing of beauty for his worship. Colin James, Bishop of Winchester, entered fully into this important day in our life, spending time with those to be confirmed, visiting the sick, and meeting and praying with the Church Council. The service of Baptism, Confirmation and Holy Communion was a most fitting context in which to dedicate the new facilities. It is full of meaning – of new beginnings and renewed commitment, all made in the light of God's love pledged to us in Christ's death. There was a great awareness that as a congregation we were beginning a new phase of our life, which would call for a new level of commitment. And the sacrificial service of our fellow men and women into which we were launching out would make sense only so long as it was undertaken in the light of God's love. Indeed, it would be possible only with a constant

awareness of his love giving us a sense of security
in what we were doing, and motivating us to cope
with the demands that would be made on us.

But we did not know very much of that when the
next morning a small group met at 9.30 to start the
Church of the Open Door's first day with prayers.
At 10 o'clock we threw open the doors and waited.
Not for long! Soon there was a steady trickle of
people. Most wanted to look round; a few stayed
for a cup of coffee and a chat. In the first few days
we were surprised by how many people living in
the neighbourhood came in just to see what we
had done with the building.

Coming through new glass doors from the porch
the visitor passes into a spacious, well-lit area
constructed of light-coloured timbers, concrete
pillars and glass. A room-height ceiling gives
an enclosed feeling, but it includes glass panels
to give a view of the west window and allow the
natural light from it into the area. On one side
a large bookstall sells Christian books, greetings
cards, music cassettes and gifts. Facing it is a
servery/coffee bar. Chairs and coffee tables are
spread around in the main space. There is a
small quiet room where those wishing to talk
privately can be taken – with narrow glass panel
windows into the main area so that those inside
can be seen though not heard – a necessary
precaution. A vestry/office and toilets complete
the new facilities.

Internal glass-panelled doors, which can be
folded right back, give an unobstructed view
of the remainder of the church right up to the
Communion table. The original serried ranks of
pews have been swept away to be replaced by

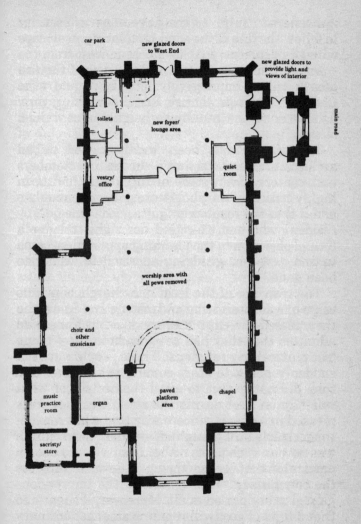

Plan of St John's after 1989 alterations

upholstered chairs. In the nave these are set out
to follow the line of the semi-circular chancel steps
created in the early 1980s. Looking west from the
worship area there is still a clear view of the full
length of the impressively lofty nave and west
window: the new lounge area, occupying only
a quarter of the building's height, is contained
within it.

The scheme has been widely hailed as an
architectural and aesthetic success by members
and visitors. Even some of those who had been
highly critical of the plans were gracious enough to
admit that the result was 'quite good'! One nearby
resident who had exercised her right to lodge a
formal objection to the planning application, came
in and gave her grudging approval to what had
been done.

The response of the local non-churchgoers who
came in was interesting and instructive. Some said
they passed the church every day, but almost all
admitted that they had never been inside – being
'not particularly religious'. These people were not
suddenly going to start coming to services; and
they did not expect to avail themselves of what
was now on offer during the week. Yet they were
pleased in a deeply sincere way that what some of
them clearly still thought of as 'their' local church
was now an open place rather than a closed one, in
particular that it was 'trying to do something for
the community'. This confirmed the impressions
gained in our parish audit. Moreover, it suggested
that a fund of goodwill remains amongst ordinary
people towards the institutional Church. It is
undoubtedly true to some extent that this is
merely the remnant of 'folk religion', but it would

be unwise to discount it altogether on that score. If we as Christians are to make any inroads into the increasingly secularised society of the 1990s, we shall have to do so across whatever bridges remain, and we shall therefore do well to take note of them. Those first few days suggested that where church buildings stand empty and locked – often for good, maybe inescapable, reasons – they spell out a stronger negative message than we have realised. Some people may feel that the Church has abandoned them, rather than the other way round.

The Bournemouth *Evening Echo* carried an illustrated feature article on the project, which generated more visits. By the end of the first week we were surprised and pleased by the level, and positive nature, of the interest shown. Around 100 people had been in, and not only to look around. Nine said they came in because they were lonely, seven 'men-of-the-road' took advantage of a free hot drink, three wanted help in finding accommodation, one was severely depressed and no less than 16 wanted to sit quietly in the worship area to think or pray. Around 30 church members had undertaken their first spell of duty as 'carers'.

Naturally, an early priority was to build up a team spirit and sense of purpose among the latter. This called for someone who could devote themselves to the task: once again God wonderfully made the right person available at the right time. Michael Jeffries had enjoyed a lifetime's association with St John's. He had served two separate spells as a churchwarden, been captain of the Boys' Brigade company and leader of

the Pathfinders young people's group. He firmly
believed that it was not good to occupy any office
in the church for too long (would that there were
more like him!); but in every one of these roles he
had made his mark through quiet dedication and
commitment. This record of distinguished service
had made him one of the most experienced and
respected members of St John's. Now here was a
task waiting to be done which called for precisely
these qualities. He had always had a strong urge
to help others, and in 1987 had taken up part-time
work with the Samaritans. His training for that
would obviously be relevant to the Open Door
ministry.

And he was available. In 1986 he had retired
early from his work as a principal revenue officer
in the Bournemouth Borough Treasurer's Department, and decided to take a year to relax and, with
his wife Betty, think and pray about avenues of
service for the future. So when he was asked to
consider becoming the manager of the Open Door
project and team leader for the carers there was
a sense in which it seemed a natural progression.
Consequently, he did not take a great deal of
convincing that this was the right job for him.
That is not, of course, to say that he wanted
to do it. Michael was one of those people whose
apparent confidence betrayed little of what was
going on beneath the surface. In fact, he felt very
apprehensive about taking it on; and during the
years that followed he frequently found himself
having to do things which he did not find at all
easy. That was Michael's sacrifice, the price which
he paid for obedience to his Master . . . and few of
those who saw him at work realised it.

So it was a terrible shock when, in the winter of 1988, after he had agreed to take the job on and he and Betty were on holiday in Italy, he suffered a serious heart attack followed by various complications. For some time there was a question mark over his ever being strong enough to do the job. Later he testified to a sense of God's presence with him through his illness, and towards the end of his time in various Italian hospitals he had a strong assurance that God would restore him to sufficient health for the task to which he had called him.

So it was with Michael as manager that the project opened, and it quickly became obvious that his administrative ability, clear thinking and knowledge of people were invaluable assets. He saw the need for simple operating systems and confidential personal records, and was able to devise and introduce them so that they were accessible to all who needed to use them. And, although his style was to lead from behind rather than the front, the quiet, calm efficiency with which he did what needed doing soon influenced the whole operation for good. He gave talks about the work of the Open Door to various groups at St John's and to other churches. As the weeks passed he developed relationships with the main social agencies in the area, and began to amass a fund of local knowledge about such things as the availability of accommodation and the dangers of getting involved with certain 'difficult' landlords!

* * *

After a few months, as the tide of seasonal visitors ebbed and autumn declined into winter, changes became apparent in the atmosphere and in our clientele, the great majority of whom were now locals. An efficient grapevine must operate amongst the less-privileged in Boscombe. News spread rapidly that here was a place of warmth and security, where you could get free tea and coffee from people who did not hassle you. A growing band of 'regulars' came in to the West End every day, sometimes all day! We started to get to know some quite well; others would never do more than sit in a corner by themselves. They all had problems, which were many and various; but there was one thing they all seemed to have in common – time on their hands, nowhere else to go, and no one else to talk to.

With the benefit of hindsight I suppose we should have expected this, but at the time it took us somewhat by surprise. We had been taught about 'availability evangelism', and this was it. The listening course had taught the carers how to empathise, identify problems and pick up signals from body-language . . . but it had not provided them with the patience and tolerance needed to cope with someone who did not actually want help, just a listening ear while they told the same story day after day. Additional supplies of grace were needed if, as often happened, the surrounding air was not altogether sweet-smelling!

There were people with more than just a chip on their shoulder. We soon learnt that those who would generally be classified as social misfits – who have personality disorders, who can never keep a job or a lodging for long, who mistrust or avoid other people – have mostly been severely damaged in their early lives. We had heard this before, and probably accepted it in a detached way.

But now we were to discover that, in order to be able to help these people, we had to listen to their story. This meant hearing about things many of us had simply not encountered before. As Michael Jeffries had told the trainee carers at a meeting three months earlier: 'You may hear some tragic, and possibly sordid, stories, and even though you may be inwardly shocked or appalled at what you hear you must try not to show it.' That was easier said than done. Some of us were discovering just what sheltered lives we had led; the world of the alcoholic, the drug addict and the occultist was not only totally alien but positively intimidating.

It may sound as if we were a bunch of dangerously amateur do-gooders. I should emphasise that all the carers were warned not to get out of their depth, nor to meddle in problems which clearly needed specialised help. The clergy and one or two very mature and experienced lay people were available when problems were of an obviously spiritual nature. A specific link was set up with a nearby GP's surgery. St John's became a member of the Bournemouth Helping Services Council, which put us in touch with around 150 specialised helping agencies in the area, so that people needing help with such problems as drug abuse, alcoholism, gambling, rape or abortion could be referred to the appropriate expert resources. Sometimes this meant befriending them by going to their appointment with them.

Some callers wanted specific help with family or relationship problems. Some wanted friends to help them rebuild their life after imprisonment, bereavement, a mental breakdown or coming off drugs. Even if they were already getting specialist

help, they often wanted to talk to someone else who
would lend moral support and who had no axe to
grind. Almost without exception they felt on their
own. *The greatest single need was for friendship*.
And this, of course, is precisely what we could
offer them, in Christ's name and for his sake.
It did not require us to be qualified specialists
or experts ... just committed, patient, tolerant,
persevering, and at times extremely courageous.
That was all! Do not think that because it was not
specialised it was easy. But we were starting to
get stuck into the task which God had for us in the
local community. At this stage in St John's life, this
was the mission to which God had called us. What
Robert Warren wrote about St Thomas' Church in
Sheffield well describes our experience: 'We have
recognised in a fresh way that being involved in
God's mission is not primarily what other people
do in other countries, but what God calls us to do
in our place.'[1] Bishop John Taylor's exhortation
in 1981 again comes to mind: 'Your new Vicar
looks to you ... to share with him both the
embodiment of God's love and the proclamation
of our experience of Christ ... and that is for the
whole neighbourhood.'

The amazing thing to us *now* is that, only a few
months previously, we did not know these people. I
do not just mean that we were not actively involved
with them. I mean we did not even know they
existed, though they were there on our doorstep,
in the gardens across the road, in the bed-and-
breakfast institutions nearby, in the bedsits that
make up much of our parish. Even had we been
aware of them, I doubt we should have thought
their presence had much to do with us. Now we

began to discover that, beneath the surface of grime, tension, anxiety or aggression, there were some gentle, caring people, able to offer friendship as well as receive it. Among those who came every day a kind of club atmosphere developed. Nobody can remember who coined the phrase, but we were soon using the term 'Westenders' as a convenient form of shorthand to describe these folk – not derogatorily, but affectionately. Nor did the use of a collective term mean we were not regarding them as individuals. They were certainly that. Let me introduce you to one or two, and you will see what I mean!

We'll call her Claire, a softly spoken woman in late middle-age. At first she was as timid as a mouse: no wonder – she later told one carer that she had 'never been a person before'. Soon she was spending every day with us, gradually beginning to relate easily to most of the carers – except for one extremely gentle elderly man, of whom she was inexplicably terrified. After a while she expressed a very simple, childish faith in Jesus . . . one of the first Westenders to do so. Soon there was no Sunday service or mid-week church meeting at which Claire did not appear, greeting effusively everyone else who came. Sadly, she now finds it more difficult to leave the home where she lives.

'Jimmy', a gangly young man of 20 or so, lives in a local authority hostel several miles from the church. His mother lives across the other side of town, but cannot cope with him. Affable and harmless, but easily led, he was (and still intermittently is) on soft drugs, sometimes hiding from the pushers. Although gullible he is by no means unintelligent. He too, soon started

appearing at either the church or St John's Centre
on Sundays, going out at least twice during the
course of a service to smoke a cigarette. He seems
to have negotiated an arrangement with a local
shop to sell him these one or two at a time,
according to the funds available!

Another regular, a stocky chap in his fifties or
sixties, has a moustache and an utterly obsessive
interest in the Scots Guards, a subject on which
he attempts to engage everyone. As time went by
he befriended, and eventually fought another man
for the affections of, a young woman who appeared
to be totally inadequate in every department of
life. She already had a little girl, and when he
announced that he was to marry her there was
another child on the way. We still see him . . . but
unhappily she is no longer with him.

Handling Westenders with mental health problems can be particularly difficult. The prize here
must go to a lady we will call Jean. For the
first two years or so she came in most days
and sat knitting furiously. Highly educated and
articulate, she was sometimes completely rational,
at others anything but! Then she would fire off
peremptory questions on everything from atomic
physics to the poetry of T. S. Eliot, expecting
the carers to respond appropriately. Many of us
felt intellectually disadvantaged! Occasionally her
vocabulary would become too spicy and she had to
be calmed down or ushered out.

This is a small, random sample of Westenders.
Added to these there were always one or two folk
who were Christians but who, because of personality disorders or other social disadvantages, had
felt less than welcome in some other churches. I do

not say we have found them altogether easy; but
it has been encouraging that they apparently felt
that St John's was accepting them as they are.

From the outset we started and ended each day
with prayers based on the ASB order for shortened
Morning and Evening Prayer. At first these were
held in the small counselling room before we
opened in the morning and in the evening after
we closed. After a few months some Westenders
began to ask if they could stay to join in at the
end of the day. Then one or two started coming
in time for prayers in the morning. After a while
it was decided that prayers should take place in
the lounge area and be open to all. Obviously
this changed their nature to some extent: in
particular it limited how far carers could detail
individual visitors' circumstances when asking
for prayer for them. But this was more than
offset by the gains. It was already remarkable
for a church of St John's tradition to be saying
the Daily Offices. That they should be said, with
apparent appreciation, by such a mixed group of
people with little or no Christian background of
any kind was quite staggering! When we reached
the time for free extempore prayer it was – and
still is – very moving to hear the prayers of some of
these folk (and that is not in the least patronising),
particularly when they pray for the leaders and
carers. They have a simplicity which both shames
and inspires us; and just occasionally they show
a flash of intuitive understanding, beside which
years of intellectual study can suddenly seem like
so much wasted time!

These are the impressions of our early days
which linger on after four years of the Church

of the Open Door. We were feeling our way;
there are some things we should do differently
if we started again today. Most of each day was
spent serving tea and coffee, washing up and
listening to people's problems. Carers spent a
good deal of time on the phone to the DSS on
behalf of clients experiencing practical difficulty,
and sometimes real personal distress, because
their benefit giro had not arrived on the due
date. Obviously there are bound to be occasional
administrative difficulties leading to this kind of
failure in the system, but the frequency with
which we were told that it was 'in the post'
ought to be a cause for concern. There seems to be
little official recognition that the person concerned
has no money at all until the cheque is received,
and that this may affect not just themselves
but one or more dependants. The line between
officials maintaining a professional detachment
from their client, and showing a cavalier disregard
for human misery and need, is a fine one. 'Most of
our visitors lived in a totally different culture from
that which seemed to be demanded by the official
structures.'[2] For many the reality is distressingly
unlike the 'caring society' portrayed by some of
our politicians.

On other days time was spent telephoning, or
taking Westenders to keep appointments with,
other caring agencies, doctors and hospitals, in
an attempt to deal with the tide of human misery
which flowed through our doors. Sometimes we
went with them to court appearances. Often,
though, at the end of the day we would have
to admit that all we had been able to do was
listen.[3] Carers often went home not just tired,

but depressed. Not everyone was able to follow
the advice to leave the day's problems behind
them. Some were giving far more than the time
they spent on duty. They were getting involved in
helping Westenders outside opening hours. Some
were sacrificing their peace of mind. Anyone who
had thought working in the West End would be a
matter of chatting to holidaymakers and explaining the pictures in the stained-glass windows had
received a shock. It was hard, unremitting work.
But it was God's work. Or was it? For some, their
tiredness was compounded by doubt.

CHAPTER NINE

WHAT ON EARTH ARE
WE DOING?

This question was fundamental to the whole enterprise. It became something we could no longer ignore – especially those who were investing a great deal of themselves in the West End. What on earth were we doing? I deliberately pose the question in those words, because behind the familiar phrase 'what on earth' lies the kernel of the problem we now had to face. In seeking to serve the community, should we be concerned with people's problems and circumstances here, or their spiritual well-being and eternal destiny? Was our ministry 'earthly' or 'heavenly'? If not the latter, then should we as Christians be doing it?

This question arises at some time and in some form in all practical Christian work. The problem that seemed to us so new and urgent in the microcosm of our West End is a global one; and it has troubled Christians through the ages because it is as old as Christianity itself. Not surprisingly, therefore, many answers have been put forward.

'Dualism' Not the Only Answer

For centuries many branches of western Christianity have embraced the concept of the world as evil and therefore something from which the Christian should separate himself. This view is usually known as 'dualism', and those holding it can draw on various Scriptures which, taken in isolation, appear to support it. Following St Augustine, the Reformer John Calvin gave it a particular twist with his doctrine of the 'total depravity' of man and the whole created order. This left its mark on Reformed Christianity generally; and although in Britain today the most conscious Calvinism is to be found amongst nonconformists, his influence historically on evangelical Anglicanism is greater than many realise – or some care to admit.

But, as Basil Hume has pointed out, this dualistic approach fails 'to recognise the unity and inherent goodness of all created things' which is, in fact, at the very heart of the Judaeo-Christian tradition.[1] To insist that the age-old question be presented in the form of 'either/or' is an unbalanced theological stance producing unnecessary pressures. It says, 'Do Christians have any business to be concerned with people's earthly existence (the "body", the "flesh", the "world"), or should they be concerned only with eternal salvation (the "soul", the "spirit", the "things of God")?' In our case the apparent antithesis was: had we opened the West End to provide people with somewhere to go and someone to help with their practical problems, or was our task to urge them towards a life-changing encounter with Jesus?

Those whose anxiety expressed itself in those
terms tended to come from this kind of *either/
or* background, which has always emphasised a
sharp divide between body and soul.

As 1990 began with a long cold spell, nobody
could deny that we were meeting a local need in
providing shelter from the weather, a listening
ear and endless free hot drinks. But the question
was asked with increasing urgency, 'But what
are we doing to present the claims of Christ on
people's lives?' It was good that some of those
working in the West End began to put the question
thus sharply. We needed someone to provide and
maintain that focus. Without it there is always
a danger that Christians engaging with people's
practical problems may lose sight altogether of
their spiritual needs. At the same time, we needed
to understand that the real question is not a
simple either/or. Presenting it in that way can
be misleading. Indeed, it can actually be harmful,
for it tends to *restrict* our vision just at the point
where, for many of us, it needs to be *broadened*.[2]

A human being is a complex creation, whose
physical environment, bodily health, relationships
and modes of thought and belief are all inter-
dependent. These various factors interact all the
time. In reality people's lives are not compartment-
alised into the things of the body and the things of
the soul. Pretending they are may be helpful to the
way we Christians like to think; but it may also prevent us from being of much use to people at all. Yet
we find it immensely difficult to learn to think in a
'non-compartmentalised' way. Not only were many
of us brought up as Christians in this dualistic mode,
but there is the wider influence of western thought

generally, which has tended to regard people's lives as comprising a number of separate divisions – body, mind, spirit, work, leisure, family and so on. The traditional approach to such things as education, medicine and work reflects this view. Society has been slow to take on board, or to work out in practice, the constant interaction between all these aspects of human life. It is now being increasingly recognised in, for example, mainstream medical practice. Unfortunately, because this holistic approach often comes today as part of a package of isms, weird therapies and Mother Earth philosophies, of which the Christian is right to be suspicious, we tend to reject also the truth that lies behind it. That is a great pity, because it is truth – and not new truth either.

The Example of Jesus

Observing how Jesus dealt with needy people, we see the holistic practitioner par excellence! He constantly showed them that, however they saw their own need, it was in fact on both the physical and spiritual level. What is more, he showed that for a person to be made 'whole' in any meaningful sense *both* levels of need must be dealt with; and, being who he was, he generally dealt with them both there and then. This is seen most explicitly in his meeting with the paralysed man, recorded in all the synoptic gospels (see e.g. Matthew 9:1–8). The man himself, the friends who went to such trouble to bring him to Jesus, and the onlookers, were all familiar with his need – to be cured of his paralysis. No wonder they were all so startled

– and, in the case of the teachers of the law, affronted – when Jesus appeared to ignore that pressing need and told the man, 'Your sins are forgiven'. But then, immediately going on to provide physical healing also, he made it plain that this was no mere by-product of spiritual forgiveness, but 'that you may know that the Son of Man has authority on earth to forgive sins'. He clearly establishes a link between spiritual and bodily wholeness. Jesus' ministry is a holistic ministry. So is his gospel. It is concerned with the whole person. But, in making such an apparently simple statement, it is important not to over-simplify: we need to acknowledge with humility that we do not fully understand this link. When the disciples asked whether a man's blindness was due to his own sin or that of his parents (John 9:1–4), Jesus' reply shows that the relationship between the physical and the spiritual dimensions is not always a straightforward causal connection.

But any caring work done in Christ's name which does not acknowledge this connection is likely sooner or later to go off the rails. It was the principle which undergirded Jesus' earthly ministry. We cannot reduce it to a simple equation; neither do we have Jesus' ability to validate it tangibly by sending paralysed people leaping off into the sunset. But neither of these is a reason to ignore it – indeed, we do so at our peril. People's physical needs are part of the whole person, and it *is* part of our Christian work to address those needs. At the very least we must show that we understand them and take them seriously.

Many of those working in the Open Door project recognised this. They knew that our Christian

responsibility to others is not 'either/or' but 'both/
and'. But recognising that does not get us off the
horns of a practical dilemma. If the problem is
not one of antithesis, it becomes one of balance.
The kind of work we were called to do involves a
balancing act. How can we keep ourselves on the
high wire?

A Question of Balance

A bedrock principle is that as Christians we have
a *spiritual* responsibility which we must never
abrogate. Any biblical understanding of the Christian faith involves acknowledging that, in the last
analysis, the needs of every person have a spiritual
origin. People are estranged by sin from the God
who made them, and ultimately our ministry must
be directed to repairing the brokenness of people's
lives by seeking to put them in touch with him in
Jesus Christ. That is our commission. Paul speaks
of God reconciling us to himself through Christ
and giving us the ministry of reconciliation (2
Corinthians 5:16–20). If our caring is to be distinctively Christian, we must be constantly aware
of that as the bottom line. That does not mean (as
John Richards had warned us) that it should be
our opening gambit. I should like to think that it
is a thing of the past for well-meaning Christians
to walk up to someone in obvious physical need
and 'challenge' them with 'Are you saved?'. But
it may be that a vestige remains if we feel a sense
of failure at not having introduced Jesus into our
first conversation with them. First we must take
the trouble to understand their need and meet
them at that point.

The concept of 'earning' the right to *speak* to people about the love of God by first *showing* them his love in action is a familiar one. Those with a special burden for personal evangelism may be inclined to dismiss it as an easy cop-out for those who find speaking about Jesus difficult. Of course, it may be that in some cases: but it ought not to be so readily discounted. The letter of James reminds Christians that to meet someone lacking the essentials of daily life, and utter comforting words to them without doing anything to relieve their immediate needs, is no Christian service at all. It merely shows that our faith is dead. (See James 2:14–18, 26.) The Apostle John said something very similar: 'If anyone has material possessions and sees his brother in need but has no pity on him, how can the love of God be in him?' (1 John 3:17). That is plain speaking!

In his teaching, as well as his actions, Jesus demonstrated the importance of recognising and dealing with people's physical needs. He ended the parable of the Good Samaritan with the simple command, 'Go and do likewise' (Luke 10:25–37). He said that even a cup of cold water (how much more a cup of hot coffee!) offered to someone in recognition that they are God's child in Christ has its eternal significance (Mark 9:41). Matthew 25 ends with a stinging indictment of those who suppose themselves to be doing God's work but ignore the practical needs of the poor, the homeless, the refugee or the prisoner. (See Matthew 25:31–46.)

In short, a balanced view of the Bible's teaching does not just make it all right for Christians to be involved in practical caring: it makes it all wrong for them not to. Yet some Christians still find

difficulty with this, fearing to be ensnared in what
they have been taught to regard as a 'gospel of
works'. The danger which they sense is very real,
and history fully justifies their fears. Some relief
agencies have departed from the Christian ideals
with which they began. So have individual Christians who felt a call to a particular social work. It is
all too easy, when we start to try and confront the
situation of the under-privileged, to become totally
absorbed by the magnitude and complexity of the
social problems we encounter. They may consume
our interest and sap our energy so that we lose
touch with the specifically Christian insight which
originally fired us. This is especially a danger
where we are campaigning against widespread
or deeply-rooted social injustice, and the sinful
structures in our society which prevent the gospel penetrating into people's minds and hearts.[3]
William Temple, who in the 1930s and 40s did
more to bring Christian insights to bear on social
issues than probably anyone else has since done
in Britain, was aware of this danger: he always
insisted that 'Christian social action' must stem
from worship and not the other way round.[4]

The Christian and Social Justice

But that is not to say that Christians should not
get involved in wider issues of social justice as well
as individual acts of caring. Again there is a strong
biblical mandate for doing so. The Old Testament
prophets saw persistent or institutionalised injustice as provoking a righteous God to anger. For
them, challenging such injustice was part of the

prophetic task of God's people. This responsibility
has to a great extent been abdicated for many
years in Britain by those parts of the Christian
tradition whose dualism has caused them to be
preoccupied almost exclusively with individual
salvation. This abdication was acknowledged by
Clive Calver, General Secretary of the Evangelical
Alliance in an interview in the *Church Times* in
February 1992, when he pointed out that 'we've
actually abhorred involvement in the secular society. We need to have a long-term commitment to
be salt and light as Jesus called us to be, to earn
the right to speak and be understood.'[5] There is
room for true repentance here.

Those who have laid such single-minded – it
might be said blinkered – emphasis on personal
salvation to the exclusion of any real concern for
applying the gospel to society at large, have been
less than true to the totality of God's revelation
about his involvement with his creatures.[6] It
has been all too easy to stand on the touchline,
clutching our Bibles, and dismiss those who are
battling it out with institutional evil as concerned
merely with a 'social gospel'. Yet Jesus himself
did not teach only the necessity of individual
acts of compassion: he also inveighed against
the hypocrisy of institutionalised oppression and
injustice in the society of his day. (See Matthew
23:23–24.) Our own experience in the Open Door
project has mirrored that of the Birmingham
inner city church (described in the remarkable
book *Power to the Powerless*), whose attempts to
combat social injustice led to the feeling that all
they could do was share in the powerlessness of
those most oppressed by it.[7]

But if the fight for social justice has been a part of the prophetic role of God's people since Old Testament times, and our Lord himself authenticated it by both his example and teaching, why do I refer to it as a danger for the Christian Church? Because it is so easy to project our personal preoccupations onto God. It is a short, often imperceptible, step from embracing a particular theology emphasising God's concern with human injustice, to adopting a belief system which assumes that this is his main, or even only, concern. In effect, this is to say, 'If God has called *me* to this work, then clearly it must be the most important thing on *his* agenda.' This is not only unwarranted (even if unconscious) spiritual arrogance; it also takes us over the line into error. *Excessive* zeal for our own particular work will have unbalanced us, causing us to slip and fall from the tightrope.

The kingdom of God concerns both individual salvation *and* human society as a whole. Both aspects must be held in tension in our belief system, and worked out in practice in a balanced way. Over-emphasising individual salvation through personal faith may fall far short of God's will by leaving a large area of Christian truth unaccounted for and a significant part of the work of his kingdom undone. Conversely, over-emphasis on the social dimension of the gospel can easily become less than Christian. The work becomes something done not so much in the name of Christ as of mere religion or eventually of humanitarianism. If those involved can no longer relate their work in any way to Christ's fundamental statement about the human condition, 'You must

be born again', it is fair to question whether it
can possibly be done in his name. Because this
danger is so real, and because it is possible to
slip into it so imperceptibly, those Christians who
are anxious that involvement in social work and
issues of justice may compromise the gospel have
good reason to be fearful.

Is it possible, then, to stay on the tightrope?
Can an urgent awareness of the need for personal
salvation be reconciled with a Christian social
conscience? Can you have a genuine concern for
people's physical needs, and yet retain a truly
Christian motivation for seeking to meet them?
And, if so, is it justifiable to serve their practical
needs *solely* as a means to 'convert' them? Even
in the abstract these are difficult questions; but
when we have to face up to them in reality, when
they dictate what we actually do and force us to
examine our motivation for doing it, they become
even more acute. But there is help. It comes not
only from the teaching and example of Jesus,
but also from church history; in particular – and
this may come as a surprise to some – from the
history of renewal. It has been a striking feature
of previous times of renewal in the Church that
the balance between personal salvation and social
action has come into sharp focus.

The Historical Perspective

In the eighteenth-century industrial revolution,
the huge numbers of people who drifted from
the countryside into the towns soon found themselves huddled together in poverty and degra-
dation. With one or two notable exceptions, the

established Church was neither sufficiently concerned nor flexible enough to respond to this new
mission field of the urban working class – a failure
from which, incidentally, it has never entirely
recovered. It fell to the Wesleys to take the gospel to them; and their new Methodist movement
ushered in a time of great renewal. Amongst many
other classic signs of renewal, this manifested
itself in obedience to the command to preach
the gospel 'to the poor', and in a willingness to
reinforce the message with a practical concern for
improving their hearers' everyday lives.

In the nineteenth century the two surges of
renewal known as the Oxford Movement and
the Evangelical Revival, although very diverse
in emphasis, had this in common: both encouraged and promoted a new breadth and depth of
social and spiritual concern. The former led to
a massive surge of church building in the inner
cities, and 'slum priests' with a strong vocation
not only to bring the poor into communion with
the Church but also to improve the provision of
schools, hospitals and housing for them. The latter
produced eminent men with a social conscience,
such as William Wilberforce who campaigned so
tirelessly against entrenched evils like slavery.

Renewal in the Social
Context Today

It should not, therefore, come as too much of
a surprise if the renewal which the Church is
experiencing at the close of the twentieth century

includes a call from God to renewed social action. In fact, one of its most public aspects has been the sight and sound of Christians coming together in praise marches to witness to what the gospel has to say to society at large. Whatever reservations some might have, the fact remains that Christians are coming out of their corner and telling the world that the gospel of Jesus and its values are relevant to modern man. Is this one sign that the awakening of the Christian social conscience is again to be a feature of renewal?

These signs are not to be found only in the charismatic wing of the Church. With the publication of *Faith in the City* in 1985 and follow-up action such as the establishment of the Church Urban Fund, the very centre of the Establishment has begun to show a renewed concern for the disadvantaged. Other unequivocal statements in recent years on social deprivation and injustice, education, the family, unemployment and business ethics, show signs that the Church may once again be becoming more like salt and light in society. These are uncomfortable commodities for the wounded and those who like the dark: the increasing stridency of those who want the Church to 'stick to religion and keep its nose out of politics' is a strangely ironical testimony to the reality of its renewal!

Yet inside our churches there are many thousands of people who would not recognise this as having anything to do with renewal. Both those who most avidly seek renewal, and those who feel most threatened by it, think of it as primarily about the individual having novel religious experiences, and Christians together enjoying new spontaneity and freedom of expression in worship.

Of course both of these are real and vital ingredients of renewal; but some appear to regard them
as the end product rather than ingredients. As a
church musician I am familiar with the notion
that, if only a church can liven up its worship
by the inclusion of some 'charismatic' songs, and
encourage its congregation to 'loosen up', it will
then be 'into renewal'! This ought to be a caricature – but sadly it is not.

This particularly up-to-date form of dualism
wants the fun of the party in the kingdom of
God without the discipline of discipleship. It is
a sign of immaturity. To offer it to outsiders as
the essence of the Christian life is, at best, to
sentence them to disillusionment sooner or later;
at worst, to mislead them about the nature of what
Jesus has to offer. This is especially tragic when
the outsiders concerned are the under-privileged
looking for something to relieve the deprivation
of their daily lives. Bishop Michael Marshall gets
right to the heart of the matter when he points out
that conspicuous charismatic renewals are often
seen where political issues are most acute and
complex. He says:

> In some charismatic over-simplification there
> is strong evidence of that dangerous doctrine
> which prescribes the slick palliative of the
> aspirin of religious experience as a substitute
> for the more costly medicine of real involve-
> ment with the needs of the world or active
> compassion for human suffering.[8]

Such instances could be said to justify Marx's perception of religion as the 'opium of the people'.

Renewed for Service

Of course, renewal will not be experienced by
everyone in the same way. We should hardly
expect uniformity from the Spirit who 'blows
where he likes'. In some places the first mani-
festations have indeed been changes in the style
and content of worship; in others the deepening
of relationships, the cleansing of institutions . . .
or in any variety of ways. But I do see signs all
around that God is today calling many in his
Church into *renewal for service*. I mean this not
only in the sense of issuing challenges and taking
action on a national or global scale, but also of a
renewed commitment to render humble service to
needy individuals. Renewal for service at this level
will be less fun for all concerned than the *renewal
of services*! It will be more demanding, and in a
number of ways, as Michael Marshall points out,
more costly. But it will perhaps be more easily
identified with the life of self-denial implied by
Jesus' call to take up our cross and follow him.
A willingness to 'lose our life' for Christ and for
his gospel may yet prove – precisely because it is
authentic discipleship – to make a greater impact
on the world in this Decade of Evangelism than
anything else the Church can do. What that may
mean for the Church corporately has yet to be
seen: but it will certainly involve being ready to
let go of much that we hold dear. 'Losing our life'
can surely mean no less, and it is part of the call to
renewal. Hindsight may show it to have been part
of the *prize*, as well as of the *price*, of following
where the Holy Spirit is leading.

I am not suggesting other churches should seek

to do the same as us at St John's. What we have done has been in obedience to what we believe was God's call *to us* in this place. But I hope our experience will encourage any congregation which hears the call of the Spirit to active social service to follow without fear. Those who have already experienced charismatic renewal need not fear that a greater commitment to practical service will mean losing their effervescence – it is more likely to add a new dimension to it. And those who have not yet experienced a new freedom in their worship, or new gifts of the Spirit, need not think themselves any less likely to experience them; a new acceptance of Christian discipline and a fresh commitment to serve Christ selflessly in the world can hardly lead to less blessing. It is the cross that releases the Spirit.

To sum up, we are called as Christians both to work amongst people and to witness to them. It is not a case of either/or. When our work, however mundane, conveys the love of Christ, it is in itself witness. *We should not doubt that for a moment, nor allow others to discourage us*. There are those whose *only* way of showing their faith is by simple, lowly service: at St John's some are doing just that. But that limitation is comparatively rare. The truth is that most of us could back up our actions with simple words of testimony, but often fail to do so through fear or embarrassment. We need to open ourselves up at this point to the Holy Spirit's enabling. The Apostle Peter said – in the context of facing the world – we should always be ready to 'give a reason for the hope that [we] have' (1 Peter 3:15).

So, what on earth are we doing, at St John's

and in other fellowships which are turning outward with a new vision for serving Christ in the
community? Simply answering the call of God to
receive *renewal for service* as a gift from the Holy
Spirit. That being so, we may expect new insights
about how the blessings we have received may be
shared with others. These insights will still have
to be worked out in practical terms – involving
down-to-earth, hard, decisions about priorities,
and in particular about how far we should go
in meeting the physical needs of those whom
we try to serve.[9] But it is no mere truism to
say that those whom God calls he also equips.
Provided such work continues to be backed by
faithful prayer, and those involved remain open
to the leading of the Holy Spirit and strive to be
true to God's word, there is no cause for undue
anxiety about falling off the tightrope.

CHAPTER TEN

OPEN DOORS ...
OPEN MINDS

We see many of our West End visitors only once, or maybe for a week or two before they move on. Sometimes we have no idea whether or not we have helped them: at other times it is obvious that we have. In his annual report for 1990 Michael Jeffries gave some examples:

A woman who had always felt unwanted and useless, and had been in and out of psychiatric hospitals. She found the carers' acceptance and friendship very helpful.

A man whose wife had just died was able to talk about her suffering, and show pictures of her, to people who really seemed interested. This helped him tremendously to work through his intense grief.

An Irishman 'on the road' after leaving home because of his wife's unfaithfulness. He was suicidal, but after three hours unburdening himself he allowed us to pray with him, and wept tears of relief. He resolved to make a fresh start, returning later to tell us he had found accommodation and a job locally.

A deeply insecure woman just out of a drug rehabilitation centre, feeling very frightened and with considerable health problems. She soon counted the carers as her only friends, and found her visits literally a life-saver.

A 24-year-old who had become a Christian in prison had left London to get away from bad influences. After ten nights sleeping rough he could not face another. We helped him find accommodation, and with encouragement from us he found a job in a hotel.

These brief encounters typify hundreds like them. They might be regarded as mere chance meetings. Yet when we pray daily for 'all those who will come through the Open Door', we believe God answers. Anne, a churchwarden and carer with particular gifts in discerning people's problems, believes some callers arrive 'by divine appointment'. One man arrived in such distress that it was difficult to find any starting point to talk with him. It emerged that he had come from Langport. It 'so happened' that Anne was on duty, that on a busy day she had just become free to go and speak to him . . . and she herself had once lived in Langport! Similar things happen too frequently to be regarded as mere coincidence.

Opening our Minds

God has enabled us to help all kinds of people with whom we had never come into contact before. But that is only one side of the story. The other side is at least as exciting, and perhaps even more

instructive. How have *they* helped *us*? Greatly
. . . especially those who, after finding help in
the West End, have stayed to become part of the
family of St John's. *Opening our doors has opened
our minds.* In many ways, without abandoning its
fundamental principles, St John's has changed
beyond all recognition. In fact, I cannot escape
the conclusion that the community's impact on
us has been greater than ours on them. Let me
try to describe some of the benefits we have gained
– some of them things most people do not even
realise a church needs. Nor did we, yet they have
greatly deepened our life.

1) The release of caring gifts

December 1991. A member of a Bournemouth
URC church decides to run in the London Mara-
thon in aid of our West End work. She writes:

> The reason why I would like to run for St
> John's is because of the great love and con-
> cern that everyone at St John's has for the
> community. At the beginning of December
> I came one morning to have coffee with a
> group of mentally-handicapped adults on our
> way to Poole to do Christmas shopping, and
> the love and patience that was shown by all
> your carers was wonderful, and was a topic
> of conversation amongst our residents, even
> after the thrill of the Christmas shopping
> was over.

This incident represents so much more. Of course,
individuals in the congregation had been looking
after others before. But it is now becoming a way
of life, sometimes for people who never believed

themselves capable of such work. A lady with a lifetime's Pentecostal Christian experience says that until the last two years she would never have dealt with the kind of people she now helps in the Open Door. Others who have always felt rather useless have found in practical service a sense of worth they had never expected. This has, incidentally, stimulated greater mutual caring *within* the congregation. (See Galatians 6:9–10.) One carer put it like this: 'We *have* to share our faith, since we can't give it . . . the Open Door is somewhere I go to be at God's disposal.' She went on, 'God has given me this ability to love . . . and shown me so much of himself through these people.' Another, after recalling some quite horrendous moments in the West End, said 'I have learnt to see the person behind the addiction. I just seem to have this great love inside me for the people who come . . .'

If you could see some of our visitors you would know that carers are not working this feeling up themselves. There is the man who deals with lice about his person by spraying them: he would rather have dead lice than wash! Or the young woman who makes continual demands, yet repays kindness with abuse and sometimes physical violence. The ability to love such people is supernatural. It is that unconditional *agape* love which God himself shows to us in Jesus. God is faithful: having called us to this work, he is equipping us for it. More and more of those who commit themselves wholeheartedly to the task of showing God's love testify that they receive a new measure of that love themselves. There is convincing, and often very moving, evidence that self-sacrifice does bring blessing.

2) The validity of non-intellectual faith

In a strongly 'teaching oriented' church there is
a tendency for everything to become cerebral.
Of course those who can should work hard to
understand the faith (see 2 Timothy 2:15); but we
must learn not to look down on those who cannot.
An influx of people with little or no Christian
background and limited intelligence is forcing
us to recognise true saving faith in which intellectual understanding plays a very small part.
This is news to some evangelicals – and not
very welcome news at that! It is a great challenge to preachers, who must stop saying 'as you
know . . .' – they don't! It requires all leaders to
look afresh at everything we do and how it is
presented. Many underlying, largely unconscious,
assumptions need to be re-examined. Attitudes
and certainties which have been beyond question
must be inspected . . . changed . . . if necessary
discarded. This is uncomfortable, but beneficial.

3) The challenge of vital Christian living

Over the years Christians can easily become
staid. Their faith sustains, but rarely excites,
them. Newer Christians have a way of innocently
puncturing such complacency. A young man in the
house group to which my wife and I belonged said
'God seems to have been telling me very clearly
what to pray for in the last few weeks . . . and
when I do he always seems to answer.' An ex-drug
user and epileptic, he still has many problems.
It would be easy to dismiss his claim as naive
enthusiasm. But it was supported with impressive detail. We had to admit that what he was
describing is no more nor less than the 'normal'

Spirit-filled life depicted in the New Testament. How often we settle for far less. The simple testimony springing from a new-found faith may uncover our half-conscious scepticism and leave us feeling ashamed of the mundane level of our own spiritual lives. And those of us who relish sophisticated theologising may find ourselves constrained to relate it afresh to the real world which the gospel both meets and challenges. Again ... uncomfortable, but good for us!

4) The value of relationships

Christians often take one another for granted. Nowadays if I go into the church several Westenders will jump up and greet me: 'Hello Derek! How are you? Is Ann all right? ... I haven't seen her around.' I hardly know some of these folk except by name; yet their pleasure is as unmistakable as an excitable puppy, and their concern genuine. Of course, they show the same interest and affection to others in the church. And despite a past full of hurt, many have a great capacity for caring and friendship amongst themselves. What a contrast with the casual, even cavalier, way in which longstanding church members can come to treat one another. This may seem a small thing, but it contains a crucial lesson. It takes folk such as these, by their unaffected delight in relationships, to provide a striking visual aid of the truth that we are all as individuals important and precious to God.

5) A diversified ministry

As the work has developed, individual carers have taken particular people under their wing to help them with quite mundane difficulties. We were

surprised by the number of adults lacking basic
literacy. They need assistance with filling in forms.
One or two have been helped to learn to read. One
carer, a lovely Christian in his early 80s, started
a regular weekly Bible study for some Westenders
who were willing to learn about Christian basics
but had no hope of doing so by themselves. He has
also become deeply involved with helping one or
two single parents, showing a loving concern which
bridges a gap of two generations! Another carer, a
hotelier, has been able to give people seasonal work.
Yet others have opened their homes to meet short-
term housing crises. There are more such things
going on than I can discover . . . not least because
those involved often wish to go quietly about God's
work without others even knowing.

6) Going out to the community

A growing awareness of needy people has led to
the development of ministry outside our premises.
The St John's Drama Group, *Southern Lights*,
began to visit prisons in Winchester, Dorchester
and Portland, sometimes teaming up with a local
Christian singing group called *Daybreak*. This is
a particularly challenging ministry although, for
obvious reasons, there is very limited scope for
follow-up, they do know that their visits have been
of significant help to a number of prisoners – as
well as being an enormous encouragement to the
chaplains. *Southern Lights* have also taken their
repertoire of Christian sketches into local schools
and colleges. Since summer 1992 they have made
a number of appearances with St John's own
music group on Bournemouth's main bandstand,
bringing the gospel to holidaymakers and locals.

Until the 1989 parish audit we were unaware that there was a bail hostel – The Pines – in the parish. After discussions with the manager, St John's began *Alongside Pines*, a small group who go into the hostel once a week to chat with the residents, get to know them and, if the opportunity presents itself, speak about Jesus and invite them along to church services and functions. The hostel's manager, initially anxious about how the relationships would be handled in both directions, says the residents look forward to Thursday evenings, adding, 'Contact with ordinary members of the local community is so important to them, especially as so many of them are estranged from family.' Soon it was decided that all those involved in visiting The Pines would act as hosts at a monthly sports evening at the St John's Centre for any of The Pines residents who wanted to come. Over games and a buffet supper it is much easier for the barriers to come down. A number of residents have started to visit the West End during the daytime, and several have attended Sunday services. Although, by the very nature of a bail hostel, these relationships can never be permanent, it is possible to sow seeds of hope for the future.

* * *

It was at The Pines that we first met Alan, a friendly Yorkshireman who had spent years driving juggernauts across the world. He had lost his HGV licence as a result of 'totting-up' penalty points for minor offences. He became a barman; but when he later applied for a publican's licence enquiries disclosed that there was a warrant out for his arrest – for non-payment of an earlier fine.

The offence having taken place when driving his truck off a ferry, he was summoned to Poole Magistrates' Court. Pending the hearing he was put on bail and sent to The Pines. Almost immediately he sensed that Boscombe was going to be a special place for him. Some of the *Alongside Pines* team told him about the Church of the Open Door and, with a bit of help from one of the other residents we already knew, they persuaded him to drop in.

Alan had a tough childhood. In a sanatorium with TB of the spine until he was ten, he emerged fearful, resentful, and somewhat bitter. He had been sent to Sunday School – his grandparents, though not his parents, being staunch churchgoers – so he was familiar with the Christian faith. But God was a threatening authority figure, waiting to punish him. As he grew up, and enjoyed the colourful experiences of an international trucker, he still tacitly acknowledged that God existed. Sometimes he even thanked God for looking after him and getting him out of the scrapes which his job and lifestyle got him into. But he wanted nothing to do with the Church: not for him the formality of religion, with authority figures thundering down at him from the pulpit.

He tells how, as soon as he came into the Church of the Open Door, he sensed that everything here was different. People were friendly. Everyone seemed to be on equal terms. They spoke to him about God's love; and one of the carers, discovering that he had no Bible, bought him one on his first visit. It was not long before Alan began to be able to envisage God as a loving Father who offered complete forgiveness and peace through Christ Jesus. Until recently he was managing to exist on social security, and helping with various practical day-to-day tasks around the church. Sadly, he has an alcohol problem, which he has yet to face up to. Despite this he is an enthusiastic witness in seeking to introduce his former friends to Jesus.

7) A challenge to 'black-and-white' attitudes

Some Christians speak of conversion as a one-off event. Even where it is, the life-changing effect of a relationship with God in Christ is gradual. This is especially true when a person comes from a background of addiction or occultism. Satan does not let go that easily. A growing desire for holiness is in constant tension with temptations to relapse into past ways. Immediate and total release from drug or alcohol addiction may occasionally happen – and it makes a very good story – but mostly it is simply not like that. *It is vital for Christians to understand this*. Otherwise they will get into an intellectual and emotional tangle about what is happening in such people's lives ... and one common way out of this is to become dogmatic and judgmental. Some examples may help to show what I mean.

* * *

The sheer scale of the alcoholism problem in society has shocked us. But there are those who at the time of writing seem to be well on the way to long-term recovery from it. Take Gillian for example. In the 1960s she was a bright university student, when tutorial changes in the third

year of her course, combined with other personal
pressures, caused her to turn to alcohol. She suffered a nervous breakdown, failed her finals, and
emerged conditioned to the idea that she was a
failure. After ten years working in engineering,
her alcoholism reached such a pitch that she could
no longer hold down any job, and she became
one of life's 'drifters'. Throughout this time she
had maintained an intermittent contact with the
Church, not least because she enjoyed singing in
choirs. Coming to St John's in 1988 she found a
welcome which she had not found elsewhere. She
soon asked if she could join the choir, where she
found acceptance and friendship which helped her
further.

She spent a good deal of her time in the West
End, where she found people who listened and
wanted to help her. The church enabled her to go
to Harne Hill, a retreat centre in the Cotswolds
where a number of our members have found real
spiritual help and healing. But her problems were
not over: in 1990 and 1991 she disappeared several
times for weeks or even months on end. Church
members occasionally reported seeing her in a
dishevelled state in the company of other alcoholics, but she was too embarrassed to acknowledge
them. She now says that she still desperately
wanted their friendship, but at the time there
was little we could do. Then in the middle of
1992 she reappeared, rejoined the choir, and has
been 'dry' ever since. That is not all. There is a
real difference about her – everybody notices it.
She studies hard, makes notes on all the sermons
and has read the lessons in church with great
beauty and understanding. One Sunday evening

she gave a spontaneous, and memorable, testimony to what God was doing in her life.

Gillian believes she has been given a second chance to make something of her undoubted abilities. She recently left us to begin a full-time degree course in Theology in Southampton. She senses God is calling her to some full-time service of Christian caring, though she does not know at this stage what form it might take. Nobody who knows her can doubt the reality of God's work in her life. But all concerned need to be aware that this does not guarantee that she may not slip and fall again.

* * *

Another recovering alcoholic who has become a valued member of St John's is Martin, a horticultural scientist and teacher whose illness cost him his marriage and very nearly his life. After intensive treatment in a specialist unit he moved to a 'halfway house', and subsequently a 'dry house' in Boscombe.[1] He felt himself drawn towards St John's as if by an unseen hand, and on coming in he knew immediately that it was God's will for him to be here. He is holding on with great tenacity, with the help of Alcoholics Anonymous and the support of friends. As I write he has been 'dry' for over two years. A lifelong music-lover, he has joined the choir at St John's, where his increasing confidence is a source of tremendous encouragement.

Martin had a knowledge of Christian things dating back to his early years. But during his period of intensive therapy he had a revelation of

God in a glorious flash of light. This unforgettable experience rekindled his personal faith and has given him a strong desire to share it with others. He attributes his 'coming to his senses' entirely to the grace of God, and can now see a golden thread of God-given life running through it all. But his past has taken a heavy toll on both his personality and his ability. Although he now has a deep faith which means everything to him and is his source of strength, he has constantly to recognise that, just as his descent into alcoholism was progressive, so too is his recovery. Living above temptation is sometimes hard work.

* * *

God is at work changing people from what they were into the likeness of his Son. That is a lifelong process for all of us. But those with the benefit of a Christian background often expect converts from a completely 'worldly' background to make the transition instantly. Californian pastor Charles Swindoll makes the point forcefully in his remarkably challenging book, *The Grace Awakening:*

> I observe an interesting phenomenon among caring Christians . . . Most of us don't require the lost person to clean up his life before he comes to the Savior. We flex, we bend, we forgive, we tolerate *whatever* among the unsaved. But we don't provide nearly as much liberty when folks come to the Savior. We don't care if they blow smoke in our faces while we witness to them. We don't even talk about it . . . 'But they had better not blow

> smoke in my face as a Christian, not if they claim to be converted!'
>
> Why not? What if that part of their life hasn't been dealt with yet by the Spirit of God? Why are we so intolerant of and impatient with our brothers and sisters? ... Think of the things in your life that are not yet cleaned up. Now maybe it isn't one of the 'dirty dozen' or the 'nasty nine' that is obvious to everyone, but think of the stuff you still have to work through ... I ask you, where is all this wonderful liberty of which Paul writes? Why do we lay such heavy expectations on each other?[2]

St Paul knew the Christian life is a battle. He described it as constant warfare between the 'flesh' and the 'spirit'. The new Christians in the churches he planted must have been constantly falling back into their old, pre-Christian ways, or he would not have needed to exhort them so repeatedly to put off the old nature and put on the new. (See, for example, Galatians 5:16–18; Ephesians 4:20–24; Colossians 3:5–10.) And he recognises that the struggle does not get easier as the Christian matures. He is himself caught up in it: who cannot identify at times with his desperate cry 'What a wretched man I am! Who will rescue me ... ?' (Romans 7: 25).

All Christians have besetting sins. The sin of pride may be overtaking the reader at this moment! Some sins can be indulged in the privacy of our own homes: the only difference may be that our repeated failures are less spectacular than those of the alcoholic or drug addict. This does

not mean they are less serious: indeed, their
very secrecy may make them potentially more
spiritually devastating.

* * *

But it is very demanding work to minister to
those in whom the battle between flesh and spirit
is particularly obvious and dramatic. When you
have invested a great deal of time and emotional
stamina in helping someone, and then they go off
the rails so publicly, it is easy to react with a touch
of self-pity . . . 'They've let *me* down'. We have had
our taste of that also.

When Stuart left the Royal Navy in 1987, having
already acquired a taste for strong drink, he began
to steal to support his habit. After a time his wife
left him, taking their two children with her, and
Stuart began a life of petty crime which eventually
landed him in Dorchester prison. In May 1991, he
was released with the clothes he stood up in, £32
in his pocket, and a rail ticket to Southampton. He
did not know what he was going to do. One thing
was certain: he would not go back to Boscombe,
the scene of his previous crimes.

Strangely, when the train stopped at Bournemouth en route for Southampton, Stuart found
himself getting off. He did not know why, and
had no real plan of action. He soon discovered
there was only one place where he had any chance
of getting accommodation. You've guessed it –
Boscombe! In a cramped, squalid room, he was
right back where he had started – no food, no ciga-
rettes, and (worst of all) no money for drink. He
went out with a half-formed plan to rob someone,

drink himself into oblivion, then give himself up.
His route took him past St John's. He had passed
it many times before but, for some inexplicable
reason, this time he stopped, read the pavement
notice, and went in. At least the coffee was free.
Soon he was pouring out his troubles to a lady
who came and sat with him. She did not try to
tell him what to do, although she did steer him
towards Alcoholics Anonymous. And she told him
simply that we wanted to help 'because we love
the Lord Jesus and are trying to serve him in
this way'. Instead of going on into town, Stuart
went back to his room. He had always thought
other people were the problem. Now he began to
realise that the problem was in himself.

Next day he went back to St John's for what
proved to be a 'divine appointment'. Someone
spoke simply to him about God's love in Jesus,
and how he could deal with our past and change
what we are. At Sunday School and naval parade
services Stuart had never heard it like this. And
he had never come across people so ready to help
others with nothing in it for themselves. That
night, back in his room, he knew something had
happened inside him. The next morning he was
on the doorstep when St John's opened. Rhys
and Gwenda Lewis were on duty, and helped
him towards the step of consciously and willingly
submitting his life to the claims of Christ.

Invited to church the next Sunday, he was
doubtful; but he came, and found friendly people,
lively singing, and a man performing a mime to a
Phil Collins record! He heard God speaking to him.
He had no idea church could be like this. Someone
prayed with him and bought him a Bible. In the

months that followed he spent a great deal of his
time in the West End, was able to help others with
alcohol problems, and appeared to be growing fast
as a Christian.

It would be great to be able to end the story
there – but, sadly, even while it seemed he had
succeeded in putting his old problems behind him,
it transpired that he was still drinking, and had
failed to meet the court's requirements following
his earlier offences. It may be that, as a fellowship,
we must bear some part of the responsibility: perhaps, by appearing to place him on a pedestal, we
had put him under too much pressure. Despite a
good deal of patient help and encouragement from
church members, he seemed unable to make any
further progress to put matters right in his life,
and eventually he stopped coming to St John's.
But we were pleased to hear that he is currently
worshipping at another church in the area, and
pray that through fellowship with them God will
deepen the work he has begun in Stuart.

Or there is the young man I introduced as
'Jimmy' in Chapter Eight. He is still very much
with us, coming to services and spending most of
his day in the West End. Listening to him pray at
daily prayers, and noting his concern for others,
one can only be impressed by what appears to be a
simple Christian faith. Yet the next day he will be
out buying drugs with apparent unconcern. What
are we to make of that?

Christians involved with such people may ago-
nise over whether their experience of God can
possibly be real in view of their behaviour or
lifestyle. But the compulsion to decide about
that, though understandable, is a mistake. (See

Matthew 7:1–5.) Our task is to help and encourage
such people; to try and build them up in their
knowledge of God; to show that we still accept
them when they fall, and to set God's standards
before them lovingly but firmly – in fact to deal
with them as God deals with us (Galatians 6:
1–5). But it is very hard to do that. It needs great
maturity and patience. It is frankly much easier
to be judgmental, and come to our own black-
and-white conclusions about their true spiritual
state. Some of us have been in the business of
doing that for so long that we have become quite
expert! But that is not what God calls us to do.
'The Lord knows them that are his'; and he is
under no obligation to share the secret with us.
True . . . that leaves us with question marks over
some parts of our ministry. But we must learn
to live with that. It is not acceptable to buy our
own peace of mind by pigeonholing people into
the 'converted' and 'unconverted'. Opening our
minds to this will involve, for some evangelical Christians in particular, a major change in
attitude.

Opening Up to Other Christians

There is one other area in which the opening of our
doors has played an important, and unexpected,
part in opening our minds. Within a few months
individuals from other churches asked to share in
the caring ministry. In ones and twos they have
gone through the training and joined the rota of
carers – four from other Anglican churches, one
Methodist, three from Boscombe's Roman Catholic church and one from a Pentecostal fellowship.

Working together has begun, at the individual level, to break down the isolation which has been one of the less happy aspects of St John's history. This is only a small beginning, but it may have major significance for the future. As Charles Swindoll writes:

> Regrettably, the stones of constraint are everywhere to be found. ... Grace scales the wall and refuses to be restricted. It lives above the demands of human opinion and breaks free from legalistic regulations. Grace dares us to take hold of the sledge of courage and break through longstanding stones. Grace invites us to chart new courses and explore ever-expanding regions, all the while delighting in the unexpected.[3]

In the past St John's has been to a large extent preoccupied with its own members and activities, guarding (somewhat fiercely at times!) the purity of its own tradition. Now we are discovering that working alongside other Christians with a similar vision and call to service brings a new breadth of mind and a new freedom of spirit.

Opening Up to God

Addressing the General Synod in 1974, Cuthbert Bardsley, then Bishop of Coventry, said that effective communication in evangelism must be firstly ecumenical, and secondly

> a ministry of humility and service. People will not listen to what we have to say unless they see us in a humble ministry of serving. And it

must be an *open* ministry; people must see us
willing to open our homes, open our pockets,
open our friendships, and open our hearts.[4]

This aptly describes our own recent experience.
For us, particularly because of our past agenda,
opening our *doors* involves first and foremost
opening our *minds* – hence my title! We have
to think in new ways about God, the gospel, and
what it means to be part of the Body of Christ in
a needy and largely unbelieving world. Now, as a
fellowship, we find ourselves beginning, through
no plan of our own, to open up in all kinds of
ways involving our worship, our relationships, our
homes . . .

As we do so the question whether to address
people's spiritual or physical needs becomes less
problematical. Experience is teaching us that the
distinction is not so sharp as some had at first
thought. And as we become increasingly open to
God, other Christians and the community, we find
ourselves thinking more about 'servanthood' and
a little less about 'soundness'. The latter remains
(rightly) on the agenda, but the former is becoming
an equally important factor *consciously* informing
our attitudes and actions. Some might regard that
as betraying true evangelical principles. Not at
all: the experience of it is quite otherwise. *The
discovery that in fact we cannot be sound without
being servants represents real, corporate growth
in grace.* God is renewing us through service.
We are still learning to understand the fulness
of what Jesus meant when he said: 'I am among
you as one who serves.' Graham Kendrick sums
it up:

So let us learn how to serve,
And in our hearts enthrone Him,
Each others' needs to prefer,
For it is Christ we're serving.[5]

Have we at St John's been helping or being helped,
finding or being found; bringing God's love to
others or receiving it afresh through them? All of
these and much more. In seeking to serve those on
the margins of society we have received at least as
much as we have given. We are learning the same
lesson as St Chad's in Birmingham:

. . . the Church must stop and listen to what
those on the margins have to teach us. Perhaps then we would begin to perceive that
those oppressed people in reality were not at
life's margins but, as Jesus saw, right at its
very heart.[6]

An anonymous verse encapsulates in a profound
way much of what I have been trying to describe
in this chapter.

In seeking to serve others –
  Do not come with compassion, but with
    desire.
  Do not come with generosity, but with
    humility.
  Do not come to bring light, but to find it.
  Do not come to gain virtue, but to receive
    glory.
  Do not come to bring Jesus Christ, but to
    embrace him.

If Christ's washing of his disciples' feet teaches
the tremendous dignity of servanthood, his accom-
panying words 'I have set you an example that you

should do as I have done for you' (John 13:15),
give a clear – indeed inescapable – mandate for
regarding servanthood as the touchstone of true
discipleship. Through opening our doors we have
received the gift of open minds and a new openness
to one another, other Christians and to God himself. Nobody would claim that we have begun to
come anywhere near the ideal of true servanthood.
But we are at least beginning to catch a glimpse of
it, to feel a yearning to strive towards it. Even that
is enough to make Satan tremble.

CHAPTER ELEVEN
KEEPING GOING

The numbers coming through the Open Door were far greater than we had foreseen. Including those coming every day, we had over 10,000 visits during 1990. Even though the carers were now often backed up by helpers brought in just to do teas and coffees, they were so stretched that they often went home feeling there had been no opportunity even to listen to anyone, let alone help them. Many felt they were no longer doing the job for which they had signed up. A few dropped off the rota; and among those who remained, the morale of some began to plummet.

At the same time people needing help with deep emotional or spiritual problems became an increasing burden. Each wanted to monopolise the attention of the person trying to help them. This desire can be most marked in those who have found a faith in God; they tend to identify so closely with the individual who has helped them to faith that they almost consume that person and drain their energy. Some wanted to monopolise several people's attention, allowing each to think they were uniquely in their confidence. In dealing with hurt people this is a common problem; but it has no easy answer. Some continuity in dealing

with troubled individuals is obviously desirable,
but we simply could not allow several carers to
get completely taken up by one person's problems.
So one or two of the most time-consuming cases
were 'allocated' to a particular carer, the others
being warned not to spend half a day listening
to the same story again. At times this seemed
hard-hearted, but it was the only way to make
responsible use of finite caring resources. And
it was made a house rule that carers should
not divulge their surname or private address
or phone number. Even this, as we shall see in
Chapter Thirteen, is not as simple to apply as it
sounds.

However hard we tried to make the best use of
resources, it became obvious that a crisis was loom-
ing. The number of those with problems requiring
continuous help and counselling went on growing,
while the 'caring time' available got less. This
increased the frustration of those carers who saw
the need, knew they had the God-given ability to
help, but were constrained by the non-stop hassle
of teas and coffees. It meant that Godfrey Taylor,
and one or two members on whom he could call
for special help with this ministry, spent more
and more time closeted with a few individuals.
The strain of this, on top of the existing burdens
of a large and growing church, began to take a
severe toll on his health. With hindsight we can
see that we were falling into a trap about which
John Richards had warned us before we started:
'Don't be dictated to by the needy, otherwise the
ministry will be swamped'.

A Year of Problems

Nor was this all. Autumn 1990 proved to be the
start of a very difficult period in our corporate
life. The events of the next 12 to 18 months
can properly be understood only in terms of a
spiritual battle. There is no doubt that the West
End's early success in meeting people's need, and
in leading new people into God's kingdom, gave
rise to a strong attack on us by the powers
of evil.[1] This was concentrated on the church's
leadership. Relationships became strained over a
number of issues, some major, but others quite
trivial; the mutual trust and rapport which had
previously existed began to disintegrate. All the
leaders felt themselves under increasing, and at
times intolerable, pressure. On occasions individual members of the team adopted attitudes and
used expressions of which we have subsequently
needed to repent.

Matters came to a sharp crisis early in 1991,
when one member of the staff team left. This
added feelings of guilt to the misunderstand-
ings which already existed about one another's
motives and loyalty. It also entailed explaining the
unhappy state of affairs to the whole congregation.
Of course, people reacted in different ways, and
for some months a deep uneasiness was apparent
throughout the church's life. If the phrase had
been coined by then, we might have called 1991
our *annus horribilis*. It is only through the grace of
God that the vital, outward-looking work to which
he had called us survived these internal stresses
and strains.

It was to be more than a year before the staff

was back to full strength. Meanwhile the effort
to keep up the momentum proved too much.
During the spring and early summer Godfrey
suffered continuous bouts of ill-health and I was
similarly affected. At the same time, one of our
churchwardens who had been receiving treatment
for cancer entered what proved to be a long and
painful terminal phase of his illness.

But more tragedy was to follow. In July Michael
Jeffries suffered another heart attack. For some
weeks he hovered between recovery and relapse,
but by October his condition was deteriorating and
he died peacefully on 14th November. The capable
way in which he had set up and begun to adminis-
ter the West End project had crowned his life-time
of devoted service at St John's. He had become
greatly loved and respected not only by those
working with him but also by the Westenders
themselves. We all knew that Michael had an
'abundant entrance' into God's kingdom. But for
us his loss was a devastating blow. The leadership
team was now two members below strength.

The seventeenth-century Scottish divine Samuel
Rutherford said, 'I see grace groweth best in
winter.' If there was one grace we needed above
all to cultivate during this period of hardship it
was the grace of patience. This did not come
easily; all of us left in the staff team are by
inclination activists. Nor can it have been an
easy time for our families – thank God for them,
especially for our wives! For the last few years
the momentum of growth and change had been
so powerful, and the sense of God's work moving
forward so energising, that the feeling of marking
time, not just for a few weeks but for months on

end, was hard to cope with. Whenever we met, expressions of frustration were interspersed with mutual and fervent reminders about the benefits of learning to wait on God! Mercifully, this period of waiting did allow time for the repair of damaged relationships.

Encouragement

The work went on. Two retired clergy helped to maintain the pattern of worship at the parish church; at the St John's Centre some 'potential' worship leaders suddenly found their potential being tested. Although this came about through a crisis, it has since proved to have been the spur which hastened the process of developing lay leadership. They attended a series of Saturday morning teach-ins at the Vicarage; and it was this group who formed the nucleus of the next phase of leadership training described in Chapter Twelve.

Meanwhile the West End, like the Windmill Theatre, never closed! But resources continued to be stretched, at times near to breaking point. The general tension was heightened in August when squatters occupied a disused URC church across the road. Often drunk and disorderly, they spent the days shouting abuse at passers-by and sometimes holding up the traffic. Several times the police boarded up the entrance only to find it torn down again the next day. These antics captured the attention of one or two of the less stable characters who frequented the West End, an alliance which obviously made us very uneasy

but which we were powerless to stop. It is a
tremendous testimony to the faith and courage
of the carers that they coped with this, on top
of being over-stretched and then leaderless. They
came through 1991 with very few drop-outs – and
newly-trained carers were being added to the rota
all the time.

Nor was the grim scenario without other encouragements. In the Open Door's early days a regular
visitor had been Max, a young man from the French-
speaking West Indian island of Guadeloupe. He
aimed to improve his English by talking to people
in the West End. Since his return to Guadeloupe
he has written to tell us that it was the pavement
notice which originally brought him in to St John's
when he was 'lost and tired'. While with us he
appeared to show no particular interest in Christian things, but he now says that after talking to
people in the West End he 'understood something'
and when he got home he accepted Jesus Christ
into his life. In a delightful letter he adds, referring
to the English weather, that 'I always say about
St John Church [sic] and some peoples I used to
meet "you've got in your heart the sun that you
don't have outside!"'

Another encouragement came from Africa. In
1989 St John's had adopted a CMS-sponsored project to build a day centre in the Ugandan village
of Guludenne. A special gift day on the opening
of the West End had enabled us to send almost
£2,000 to this project. The same year we had sent
four able-bodied people (at least they were when
they left Bournemouth!) to Guludenne, along with
others from Christ Church, Winchester. Some
laboured on the building site; some encouraged;

they all got involved in street evangelism. This
had proved very worthwhile – not just for the
people concerned but as a demonstration that our
renewed concern for the people on our doorstep
did not have to be at the expense of Christian
causes further afield. Subsequently Simon and
Doudie, the two young men who had planned
the day centre in Guludenne, paid us a return
visit. Neither had ever been outside their own
country before. What a shock Bournemouth must
have been to them . . . not to mention the English
weather! As they left we were amazed to hear
them say *they* were challenged by *our* West End
to ask themselves how they could serve God more
effectively in their own community. Once again we
felt encouraged and humbled at the same time.

In December 1991 a short BBC1 local news
feature on our West End work led indirectly
to further encouragement from as far away as
Canada! The Rector of the Church of St John
the Divine in Victoria, British Columbia, hearing
about the Church of the Open Door from a relative
who had visited us, wanted to know more. We
sent a copy of the BBC programme and a video
of a typical All-age service at St John's. It was
shown to various groups in this large Canadian
urban parish, who were said to be impressed
by the 'terrific outreach and the caring-without-
forcing Christianity' in the Open Door. They also
commented on the 'high energy level, freedom,
numbers of children and mixture of grey hair and
youth' in our worship. More important still, this
contact prompted an examination of their own
community outreach, and we heard in 1993 that
major initiatives were being planned to increase

the effectiveness of their outreach to, and service in, the local community.

Changed Lives

Nor, despite the difficulties I have described, was the ongoing work at St John's without its encouragements during this period. One came on a Sunday morning in the summer of 1990, when the service at St John's Centre had been planned to include an invitation for anyone present to speak briefly about what God was doing in their life. This is a very open-ended (not to say risky!) thing to do, and when a bespectacled man in his mid-30s, whom hardly anyone knew, stood up and said that while doing a paper round he had seen a vision of Armageddon, the leader wondered what was coming! But what followed had such a ring of truth about it, nobody doubted the integrity of what they heard.

Neil had always been something of a loner. As a teenager he was an avid reader of horror stories, fascinated by their references to hidden knowledge and ancient scripts. By the age of 18 he had found others with similar interests and was besotted with the whole subject. Never having felt in tune with the rest of the world, he began to have a greater sense of belonging in this realm of dark, hidden things. Leaving school and starting work, he looked like a 'normal' commuter, but beneath the surface lurked an urgent desire to escape into the world of the occult, there to exercise what he felt were his own latent magical powers. But, dimly aware of the power of the forces involved, he was in fact too frightened to practise what he was learning. Although he drifted away from the occult for a few years the tensions increased, and by the age of 30 he was being treated by doctors for nervous strain. He turned back to it again, hoping it would provide an escape from his problems. If it did not he even contemplated entering a monastery. Neil was on the edge of a breakdown.

Moving to Bournemouth he met and married a vivacious and intelligent girl called Louise. Life now held new charm and excitement. But Louise's own inner life was a vacuum waiting to be filled. With no Christian family background, she had visited several churches as a youngster, but felt nobody was interested in her. Still convinced that there was 'someone or something there' she had a deep sense of searching. No surprise, then, that on discovering Neil's occult interests, she thought 'this is it'. Together they took it up, Neil with greater enthusiasm and Louise as a keen learner. They discovered that what had previously been 'under the counter' was now freely available . . . astrology, rune reading, witchcraft and various ideas and activities under the general New Age banner became part of their daily lives. Many had an apparently beneficial ecological slant; this particularly appealed to Louise, who was anxious to be thought of as a 'nice person with a desire to save the world'. Soon her new friends were telling her she was a natural. They duly celebrated the pagan festivals with the appropriate magic ceremonies. They were happy in what they were doing but, looking back, never fulfilled. Neil still

hungered for power; Louise was still conscious of
searching.

In 1988 Neil learnt about a new branch of the
subject known as 'chaos magic': freeing participants from the need to celebrate the festival
rituals, it offers particularly potent personal powers. Unusually, for some reason it did not seem
worth carrying out the winter solstice ceremonies:
they were on the brink of something new and even
more exciting. One evening, as Neil sat in their
lounge undergoing a 'dream journey', he saw a
man on a donkey riding up a hill. He did not
know who it was but, going into the next room
where Louise was meditating, Neil took out the
personal diary recording his magical experiences,
tore out all the completed pages and found himself
writing on the next page JESUS CHRIST IS THE
ONLY GOD. He had no idea why he was doing
this. Louise was profoundly disturbed.

It was shortly after this that Neil was out
delivering free newspapers when suddenly – he
describes it as like a television being switched on –
he saw Armageddon, the final battle between Good
and Evil. Satan appeared to be expressing surprise at the ease with which Evil had triumphed,
when a shining light appeared, heralding a figure
with an angel on either side of him, each carrying
a banner. Neil recognised the figure instantly.
It was the man he had seen on the donkey;
he rebuked Satan and told him that he, Jesus
Christ, was the victor. The vision faded, and
Neil found himself alone on the street with his
bag of newspapers. It was a cloudy day, but
at that instant the clouds parted and the sun
streamed down straight onto his face for only a

couple of seconds, then disappeared. He had, quite literally, seen the light! Naturally he wondered what it all meant, but there was no immediate powerful emotional reaction. As he worked near Christchurch Priory, he started going in during his lunchtimes. He felt sure he should pray, but did not know what to say to God. Eventually he acknowledged that what he had been involved in was wrong, and said he was sorry. He began to pray and to read his Bible daily at home. He did all this in secret, feeling he was somehow letting Louise down. After all, it was he who had led her into occult paganism . . .

This went on for over a year, until at Easter 1990 he woke up with the single thought in his mind 'I'm going to church'. He told Louise, who would have none of it. Neil left the house, not knowing exactly where he should go. Then he remembered St John's . . . he had once seen the pavement notice and gone in; on that occasion he had stood at the bookstall, but then his nerve deserted him and he had fled before anyone spoke to him! But he had felt it to be a place where people were made welcome, so it was to St John's that he now went. After the service the Vicar spoke to him, and Neil told him briefly what had been happening in his life. Godfrey's response was 'I think I'd better come and see you'. A visit followed, in which Louise remained unmoved. Anxious to establish that she was a 'good person' rather than a bad witch, she nevertheless wanted it to be understood that she was doing what she did because she believed it; she was not going to be dragged wherever Neil led. But she did start going to St John's Centre with him on Sunday mornings, and

agreed to attend a midweek discipleship course
to help her understand what was affecting Neil.
On the fourth week of the course the message of
the Christian gospel suddenly hit her, so hard it
was inescapable. She could stop searching and
striving, just take what God was offering and be
herself. She describes it as like the lifting of a
great weight. After all these years she knew she
had found what she had been searching for.

Of course, the going is sometimes hard, but Neil
and Louise have never looked back. There is a
great deal they have had to give up, but in its
place they have a peace and a sense of purpose.
Neil no longer wants to escape from life but to
live it. Louise is now keen to learn, but does not
have to search. They both know that in finding
Jesus they have acquired the 'pearl of great price'.
On becoming a Christian Louise was amazed to
discover that a cousin had been praying for her
for 12 years. Later on Neil was equally amazed to
find himself telling his story to over 1,000 people
at a celebration in Winchester Cathedral. They
have become stable Christians with a mature and
balanced grasp of Christian truth, and are both
now training to become home group leaders.

The Waiting Ends

For the church as a whole, the sense of waiting
which had pervaded 1991, began to ease with the
dawn of the new year. At last it looked as if the
rebuilding of the staff team was beginning. Simon
Foulkes, coming to the end of his first curacy in St

Austell, Cornwall, was looking for a parish where
he could be responsible for a daughter church.
He and his wife Anne had explored several possibilities, and had been perplexed and somewhat
frustrated when for various reasons none of them
worked out. Now they received details of the job to
be done at St John's, and after several discussions
it was decided that, with their children Thomas
and Claire, they should join us at the beginning
of April 1992. Simon would have personal charge
of the congregation at the St John's Centre, with
special responsibility for training and the development of lay ministry.

At the same time as he arrived, the church
secretary/ administrator retired. The decision was
taken to combine the administrative side of the
job with that of manager for the West End, still
vacant after Michael's death. So began the search
for somebody with the required blend of people and
administrative skills. Before advertising the post
externally it was decided to give church members
the opportunity to express interest, and several
did so. After some heart-searching it was decided
to appoint Chris Hawley. Chris was at that time
a churchwarden; during the mid-80s he and his
wife Lindsey had been leaders of Spectrum, the
church's under-30s group. After spending nine
years in the regular Army he had taken up free-
lance photographic work, later becoming a tech-
nician, then a lecturer, in that subject at the
local College of Art and Design. He had felt for
some time that God was calling him to leave
this profession behind and take up some form
of full-time Christian work: and as they prayed
about it together he and Lindsey had a strong

conviction that it was in Boscombe that this should
be fulfilled.

An action-man rather than a deep thinker;
preferring to be on his feet (or his bike!) than
at a desk, Chris was not in some respects the
obvious choice for this combined administrative/
caring task. But by now we were beginning to
recognise a pattern in the way God met our needs
for key people. Julie Maddams for the playgroup;
Rhys & Gwenda Lewis for the listening course;
Michael Jeffries to start up the Open Door project
. . . what was it they all had in common? They
sensed a call from God; they prayerfully overcame
any doubts about their suitability; they made
themselves available; they were ready to make
sacrifices. Here was a similar pattern again. The
task matched the call to Christian service which
Chris had been sensing for some months before
the job even existed. He was prepared to follow
the call, even though it meant giving up his career.
It would involve sacrifice – the church could not
afford to match his existing salary, so it would
be a step of faith for him and Lindsey, with two
small but rapidly growing children. In the light of
all this we felt confident that he was the man, and
he decided to take the job from September 1992.

This left some months during which the West
End project would have to continue without a
manager, and developments there continued to
cause concern. How we wished we still had Michael
Jeffries' wisdom and sensitivity. The original
vision had been of a peaceful place where people
could talk over their problems or just sit quietly.
Carers were trained to listen; their ministry was
to offer friendship, give practical help and share

their belief in Jesus Christ. But we had allowed
ourselves to be sidetracked. It was becoming a
cafeteria, whose most distinctive feature was
that it was free! This was its attraction for
large numbers of people, many of whom had
no real wish to talk or find friendship. The
demands of serving refreshments and clearing
up after people (mostly not over-clean in their
personal habits) were absorbing the carers' time
and energy. Even if they had time to talk with
people, the level of noise and bustle, sometimes
bordering on disorder, was not at all conducive
to listening. Timid, insecure visitors needed to
relax and feel safe before they could start to share
their problems. Now people could sometimes be
seen hovering in the doorway and, on observing
the company and the atmosphere, walking away
again.

Some carers felt defeated by the problems. With
hindsight, the church leaders should perhaps have
made exceptional efforts to maintain close and
regular communication with carers during this
period; but we had been without a curate, administrator or secretary and there were many other
pressures. By early summer 1992 the impending
crisis could not be ignored. It was decided to
restrict tea/coffee to a one-hour period each morning and afternoon. The West End should also close
for a few minutes in the middle of the day, encouraging the morning and afternoon shifts of carers to
have a 'handover' and pray together. These measures certainly helped produce some quiet periods
during the day. Conversely, while refreshments
were being served the problems were intensi-
fied. A very rough element adopted us as their

meeting place, huddling together in one corner. They plainly resented anyone approaching them, ceasing their conversation abruptly; we were not at all sure what deeds were being plotted. At times the atmosphere could only be described as intimidating.

Chris Hawley had talked to carers about this during the summer, and had thought and prayed about it; so on taking up his post in September he was ready to act. Allowing things to go on as they were amounted to changing the vision we believed God had given us for the Open Door ministry. The refreshments had to go – completely! It was a hard decision; carers' opinions were, naturally, divided. Some days were now so quiet that people who had given up time to be on duty wondered if it was worth it. Others, however, could see the benefits, which Chris has summarised as:

– a greater sense of peace in the West End than there has been for some time;
– people communicating more fully and openly;
– the Bible being opened by those on duty to answer questions from visitors without a Christian faith;
– reduced stress on carers, increasing their ability to cope when difficult people/incidents do arise;
– those really needing companionship or help still coming in and getting them.

Experience shows that, although far fewer people are coming into the West End, the quality of the time spent with those who do is far greater. Periods of apparent inactivity are increasingly being used

to deepen relationships – both amongst carers
themselves and with those of the Westenders who
are now very much church members.

The Cornerstone – A New Ministry

A spin-off from this decision led to a new area
of ministry. Coming just before the winter, it
provoked a number of carers to consider whether
we could not do something else to demonstrate our
practical concern for those lacking life's essentials.
It was decided to open the Selwyn Hall between 12
and 2 p.m. every Tuesday to serve a free bowl of
soup and bread roll to all comers. A few members
got together to plan and pray. Soon they had
received a freezer, several gifts of money, six trays
of canned EEC meat and the offer of a regular
supply of free rolls (and often cakes) from a local
bakery's surplus production ... and promises of
help from church members. The *Cornerstone* ministry was born.

1.15 p.m. on the first day saw us rushing out
to buy tins of soup! The level of demand took
us completely by surprise, and our home-made
supplies had quickly run out. The next week we
made twice as much. By Christmas an average of
90 people were coming in, and by May 1993 this
had reached 150. Church members are invited to
come when they can, and to try to get alongside
the people there. This is the most challenging
part of the operation. With the Westenders who
we already know, it is not too difficult. But others,
homeless or on the road for other reasons, are
often solitary by nature or conditioning, and not

necessarily very keen to talk. It is hard to steer
a course between providing a welcoming, family
atmosphere and forcing our attentions on people
who only want the food. But it is vital, because
once again there is a balance to be struck. It *is*
a worthwhile – and Christian – ministry in its
own right to meet people's physical needs; but
our awareness of their spiritual needs forbids us
to ignore them. The *Cornerstone* is a God-given
opportunity to combine the two.

On a practical level it is quite an undertaking . . .
collecting food, preparing vegetables, making and
serving soup, laying and clearing tables. Although
some of those involved were already carers in the
West End, other church members have rolled
up their sleeves to do things like washing up,
extending still further the numbers of those on
active service. For some time one of the men from
The Pines bail hostel has conscientiously laid up
the tables. The *Cornerstone* is also strengthening
relationships with other churches. The Lansdowne
Baptist Church, who had previously run a similar
venture, gave a great deal of valuable advice and
help in getting us started; and they and friends
from Winton Baptist Church in Bournemouth are
instrumental in procuring food supplies. They and
members of other local fellowships offer practical
help and prayer support.

For those involved in this ministry, Tuesday
has become a very special day. A time of prayer
and sharing together at 11.30 a.m. has become
very precious, and provides a powerful spiritual
launch pad as the doors are thrown open and
the hungry multitudes pour in, unaware of the
secret ingredient that goes into their soup . . .

the recipe reads 'Add half an hour of heartfelt, believing prayer, and serve with a seasoning of fresh Christian fellowship'!

Moving Ahead

By the end of 1992 the team was back up to numerical strength. Moreover it soon became apparent that God had brought us people with complementary abilities. Chris Hawley's practical skills and down-to-earth approach lightened the administrative load on many shoulders, notably Godfrey Taylor's. Simon Foulkes quickly made his mark at the St John's Centre as a capable leader, teacher and encourager, with particular ability to develop the potential in others – which must be a priority if an expanding church is not to outgrow its own strength. And he proved to have a mind which was creative yet analytical (a rare combination!), allied to administrative know-how developed in his early career in junior management with British Rail. He was clearly going to be a forceful and stimulating colleague.

There was no mistaking the fact that the ship which had been becalmed for so long was at last on the move. But it was not long before God's hand was again felt on the wheel. We were undergoing yet another change of course.

CHAPTER TWELVE
THE WAY AHEAD

The year 1992 began with

- fresh hopes of the arrival of a curate;
- plans for extending our facilities to enable us to think more adventurously both about serving the local community and reaching out to those with no knowledge of the Christian faith;
- some burgeoning ideas about the possibility of a town-wide mission to coincide with St John's centenary in 1995.

With vital developments expected on these three fronts, Godfrey Taylor nominated it 'This Crucial Year', and set out the exciting prospects in a 'mission statement' given to every member of the congregation:

In the event 1992 certainly proved crucial, sometimes in ways which we could not foresee. As I have already indicated, the arrival in April of Simon and Anne Foulkes quickened the gentle movement of the ship which we had detected at the beginning of the year. Soon the bells in the engine room could be heard ringing 'full ahead' in

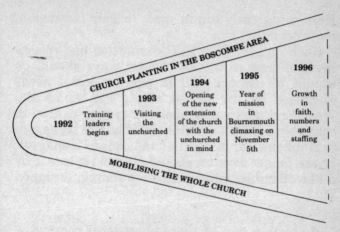

Mission Statement

some direction or other almost daily! The familiar
territory in which we had been becalmed started
to slip away rapidly.

The Future of the Selwyn Hall

The Selwyn Hall was originally built in the 1890s
(in six weeks!) to house the newly-formed congregation while the church building was being
erected. Older St John's members feel an understandable affection for it; but fresher eyes see a
shabby, uncomfortable relic of a past era. It is
still used for community activities like jumble
sales, plant shows, English language classes for
overseas students, blood donor sessions – and as
a polling station! But since the Centre opened
in 1985 the church's own use of the Selwyn

Hall has greatly diminished, largely because of
its inflexibility.

Back in 1989/90 a PCC committee had recommended that in the *short term* ways should be
sought to use the hall to address social needs
identified by the parish audit, and which the
West End could not meet ... maybe a drop-in
centre, lunch club, evening coffee bar for teenagers
or clubhouse for mentally-handicapped teenagers.
In the *longer term* we should plan to replace it by
a new, flexible, multi-purpose building, designed
to:

• enable any of these short-term community initiatives which had proved successful
to continue;
• provide a good-sized hall for public events;
• expand the church's facilities (for example
a purpose-built creche and ancillary meeting
rooms);
• utilise any spare space (they envisaged
a three-storey building) to provide much-
needed affordable rented accommodation for
church members or others.

After much discussion the PCC concluded that:

• we should not stimulate new uses for the
existing hall but proceed straight to planning
a new one;
• it should provide facilities for extension
of the Open Door ministry, the use of the
church family and the community generally,
including in particular a new playgroup;

- the provision of residential accommodation on any worthwhile scale was not feasible.

A local architect produced an outline which was then developed into a detailed design. A most attractive scheme, it caught the imagination of church members, and came unscathed through the processes of diocesan consultation and local authority planning consent.

It was obviously going to involve an enormous financial challenge. But as the majority of four-year covenants made by church members for the West End project would expire in 1992, it seemed a propitious time to call for further sacrificial giving to enable us yet again to 'see people through buildings'. Even so, when the estimate of £600,000 came in there was a sharp intake of breath! Few members had not been affected in some way by the recession; in a number of families the main bread-winner had lost his or her job. And, although our membership had been growing, a significant number of the newer members had come in via the West End; in the nature of things they were unable to make a significant financial contribution. Nevertheless, we could not forget the lessons of faith from the two major projects of the 1980s, when God provided remarkably for our needs through his people's generosity.

Congregational meetings were called to describe the project and its aims, and those present confirmed their wish to go ahead 'in principle'. So a Sunday was set aside in October 1992 for members to pledge their support. The leaders had decided that at least £300,000 needed to be pledged for us

to be confident that God was calling us to go ahead.
Pledge Sunday produced promises of £177,000. I
avoid the word 'only' because, in the prevailing climate of recession and economic uncertainty, this
was a truly magnificent response. But it was not
a mandate to go ahead. An anxious, but prayerful,
period followed while various ways were examined
of cutting or spreading the cost without reducing
the facilities.

Sermons during January 1993 concentrated on
the whole subject of sacrificial Christian giving –
a worthwhile exercise in itself! At the end, our
annual 'Commitment Sunday' was used to ask
everyone to reconsider their pledge to the project
in the wider context of the church's operating
budget for the year ahead – which also needed
a £30,000 increase in giving for the existing work
to be maintained. Again members responded to
the potential budget shortfall in a way that can
only be described as magnificent; but, so far as
the project was concerned, the amount pledged
was still insufficient to go ahead.

Naturally this was disappointing. But it would
be quite wrong to allow disappointment to develop
into a sense of failure. Although the vision for this
project may have been slightly less clear than on
previous occasions, throughout its planning we
were corporately seeking God's will for developing
his work. The response of faith is to believe that
the outcome is indeed his will. The widespread
enthusiasm for the scheme, and the congregation's
generous response, are very positive factors. Many
feel it was the right project but the wrong moment;
time may well prove that the signal God gave us in
1992/93 was amber rather than red.

Mobilising Potential Leaders

Meanwhile, on the people front, very positive
things were starting to happen. During 1991, with
the full-time staff depleted, several members had
taken increasing responsibility for leading worship and teaching at the Centre. Simon Foulkes
now invited some of them, and a number of other
members, to undertake more intensive training
using the Oak Hill Extension Course (OHEC).
This would involve a major commitment of time
and energy, so they were encouraged to drop
other responsibilities in the life of the church.
This is important. The people with real leadership
potential in churches often have busy lives and
responsible full-time jobs with their own stress
factors. It is right for the church to ask for commitment . . . but wrong to expect so much of able
people that they are placed under harmful stress,
to the possible detriment of their health, families
or paid employment. That is *not* good stewardship
of the human resources of God's kingdom. It is not
always easy for full-time parish clergy, whose way
of life is essentially different, to appreciate this.

This initiative was designed not only to equip
them for leadership at St John's Centre, but also
with an eye to the longer-term. The Centre was
now bursting at the seams every Sunday when the
youngsters joined the adults for all-age worship.
Up to 300 people regularly crowd into the main
hall which can only comfortably accommodate
around 250. In some ways this is tremendous
fun; but it makes the task of worship leaders
very difficult, severely curtailing the scope for
activities such as drama, mime or dance. And

growth continues. This points to the need to plant a new church – to which I shall return later in this chapter.

Reaching the Unchurched

A major component of the OHEC course involved theoretical and practical work in visiting the unchurched. Early in 1993 each course member, supported by members of house groups, visited a number of homes in the parish. What they found corresponded in many ways to the parish audit in 1989. Although there was a more obvious layer of suspicion, and sometimes fear, to penetrate, people were generally quite forthcoming about themselves, and for the most part pleased that someone from the church was taking an interest in them. A surprising 17 per cent were thought to be open to a further visit – and we do not think they were saying this just to get rid of us!

To follow this up as a way of making significant new contacts with the unchurched people of our parish would require considerable mobilisation of resources, and call for new levels of commitment and courage from a large number of members. There is a strong temptation to draw back. It would be easier to bring our friends from work and the comfortable neighbourhoods where we live (although many of us have not yet done even that!). That would be a more 'efficient' use of resources – and of course it would be worthwhile; every soul won for Christ causes rejoicing in heaven. But it would be to perpetuate the past pattern of an electic church without roots in its parish and community. I believe it would be to

turn our back on the new *vision* and new *call* God
gave us during the late 80s. We are struggling with
this as I go to press.

Back in 1988, when the builders were about to
move into the West End of the church, Godfrey
Taylor wrote that our door needed to be open –

• for needy people to *come in* and find
friendship and help;
• for the worshippers to *go out* with a
living practical faith into the surrounding-
community.

God has enabled us to make some progress on the
first of these in the last four years. By showing
practical care and concern for those who come
in through the Open Door we have begun to
commend ourselves to the people of the area.
A number are now church members; some have
found faith in Christ for the first time; others are
being helped towards it. But the second remains
for the most part unfulfilled. There are many
who will never come in, because they do not have
the Westenders' practical and emotional needs.
Of course, they have a desperate spiritual need,
but are quite unaware of it. We must not draw
back from the call to go out to them with the
gospel of God's love in Christ. Hence our 'motto'
for 1993: '. . . to preach the gospel where Christ
is not known . . .' (Romans 15:20).

Here we start to get into the realm of the
unknown future. But there are two initiatives
which might be developed into in-depth evangelism of the local area – either separately or
together.

Church Planting – A Pastoral Plan for Boscombe

It is not only the overcrowding problem (if that is the right word!) at the Centre which prompts us to consider planting a new church. There are other cogent reasons:

- The Centre congregation – itself only part of the total St John's congregation – has outgrown the size at which church-growth experts consider pastoral care and evangelistic effectiveness reach their limits.
- It is strategically appropriate. Soon after becoming Archbishop of Canterbury, George Carey emphasised that every church should be seeking to plant another.
- Most compellingly, God has been bringing to our attention the challenge of the 'unchurched'.

With potential leadership resources for a new congregation already being prepared, the urgent need is to identify and gain the use of suitable premises in which it could meet. A search within our own very restricted parish has produced no realistic possibilities. Church planting *across* parish boundaries is an emotive subject, which has more than once hit the headlines recently. The parochial system may have served the Church of England well for 1000 years or more; but in today's context its rigidities can sometimes be a real hindrance to the spread of the gospel.

The relationship between manpower and demand for the 'product' in the Church is not the same as that which exists in industry. If it were, demand would currently justify vastly *increased* manpower! As people's problems mount with falling employment and widening gaps in society, the Church's 'product' – that is, the gospel of every individual's worth as a person created and loved by God – is more desperately needed than ever. Yet, ironically, the Church is subject to the same economic pressures as a business in terms of meeting costs of staff, buildings and administration. But it cannot just lay off its workers, or make them redundant. In these circumstances it is essential that the most effective possible use is made of the resources that are available. This will involve examining critically, and tackling courageously, not only the rigidity of parish boundaries, but also the financial drain of historic but pastorally inappropriate buildings and the unwarranted luxury (I write as a layman) of the parson's freehold. These are difficult, complex and inter-related issues; but if evangelism is to be a genuine priority in this decade they will have to be tackled urgently and radically.

In the 1990s Boscombe is no less affected than anywhere else by considerations such as these. Thus it was that, during 1991/2, the Diocese had already asked the Bournemouth Deanery to draw up proposals to rationalise the staff and buildings in various areas of the town. The Deanery recognised that, in Boscombe, these should take into account the scope for adjusting parish boundaries; the need already established to plant a new church; and the opportunity afforded by the retirement of incumbents in both St John's neighbouring parishes to introduce a coherent strategy for the Anglican Church's work in the whole area. This ought to involve some kind of 'partnership' – at working level or possibly in a more formal way. It is not possible at the time of writing to say how this might develop. What does seem clear is that this approach would greatly assist both ministry and evangelism in the area; and, conversely, that failure to put some such plan into effect would be an opportunity lost.

A Church for the Unchurched

For the last decade at St John's we have been consciously working to make our worship 'user-friendly'. Especially at the St John's Centre the style is essentially informal, the music mostly modern, and the teaching often participative rather than 'tell-and-sell'. This approach stems from the personal convictions of the leadership, but it also responds to the comments in the 1989 parish audit (and, before that, *Faith in the City*) about the importance of making worship 'accessible' to those who come.

But in the last year or two we have become more aware that increasing numbers of people in our society have no Christian knowledge or background whatsoever. For the first time in Britain we are dealing with a generation many of whom have not experienced school assemblies with a Christian content. These are not people who have rejected, or even ignored, Christianity. In 1990s Britain they have simply never encountered it. To such as these even our most informal, user-friendly acts of worship would be totally alien. In fact, we have begun to doubt whether it is right to get them to a service including worship songs with which they cannot possibly identify and prayers to a God of whom they have no concept. The more astute among them might see this as asking them to forego their intellectual honesty. The rest would just know they felt distinctly uncomfortable. Rather than inviting them to participate in acts of worship, should we not be 'presenting' the gospel to them in a more objective way – making particular efforts to start from a point which is relevant to people's everyday lives?

Some readers will know that this approach has been explored in America in recent years – notably at Willow Creek.[1] A number of churches on this side of the Atlantic have tried to put the principles into practice in a British context. Probably the best-known example is the 'Nine o'clock Service' at St Thomas' Church in Sheffield.[2] We are exploring this whole area. A 'pilot' presentation at the St John's Centre in April 1993 under the title 'If Only . . .' took relationship problems as its starting point. Partly to show the church family what is in mind, and partly 'for real', it filled the Centre and was well received by our visitors. A series of such *seeker-targeted* events, to be held on Sunday evenings once a month, is being planned for 1994. This may mean changing the worshipping habits of a lifetime for the existing congregation on those weeks – possibly

holding the main evening Communion service
midweek.

The Way Ahead

How does one end an unfinished story? The events
of the last year suggest that God may be leading us
to concentrate on the development of our human
resources, to prepare us for what we are beginning to sense is a fresh call to mission. Valuable
practical experience was gained by several of our
men who took part in the Walk of 1,000 Men in
autumn 1993, which involved them in evangelism
in streets, homes and pubs throughout Cornwall.
If God is driving us *out* through our Open Door to
those who will never come *in* of their own volition,
that will call for a deepening of our own spiritual
lives and a new level of commitment. Over a period
I have kept coming back to a passage in Ephesians
Chapter 4 in this context – and the speaker at our
1993 PCC Study Day took it as his theme too! Paul
writes about the gifts which Christ apportions to
his people. In verses 11–13 he speaks of various
gifts and ministries, putting them in the threefold
context of

- works of service
- building up the body to maturity
- unity

1 Works of Service
Nobody who has been involved at any level with
the work going on in the West End has any

doubt that it is God's work. There is a constant
stream of testimony from regulars, casual visitors
and carers, of the ways in which he is using
and blessing it. We must not stand still. We
must constantly be on our guard against complacency. We must seek to continue to develop
it as resources allow, remaining open to God's
leading.

2 Building up the Body

Developing the West End work, together with a
new and growing emphasis on mission, will need
greater (not less) effort on looking after the body
of existing believers. Pastoring a church of 400
plus members is difficult. The familiarity of that
statement makes it no less true. It is a formidable
problem, and a daily dilemma for the leadership.

In any large church identifying, harnessing and
developing the many and varied gifts of members
ought to be a No. 1 priority. While those with
the more obvious, up-front gifts have usually
been seized upon eagerly, there remains a pool
of people willing and gifted in the area of pastoral
care. It takes discernment, patience and a great
deal of time to find them and mobilise them.
But to leave them under-utilised represents a
major, corporate failure to employ gifts given by
God for the good of the Body. There are many
churches which would give their right arm for
just one such person! A truly effective pastoral
team can be expected to have a 'ripple' effect
throughout the entire membership – people who
are more aware of being looked after themselves
can become a broader, firmer and more motivated
base for outreach into the community.

One member with strong pastoral gifts felt
strongly for some months that God was calling
her to new work in this area. No sooner had
she shared this call with the leadership than she
suffered what was thought to be a coronary. We
could not help being reminded of the way in which
Michael Jeffries had suffered a heart attack after
agreeing to take on the management of the West
End. Once again we asked ourselves whether we
were encountering spiritual opposition because we
had set a course which has great potential for the
progress of the gospel.[3] Happily in this case it
was subsequently confirmed that, although her
illness was a serious viral infection, she could
expect eventually to make a full recovery.

Home groups are, of course, a recognised way
of achieving pastoral care within a congregation. We are currently carrying out a major
review and restructuring in this area, planning
far more extensive training for home group leaders. They will then be given greater, and more
explicit, pastoral responsibility for the members
of their groups. A proposed new Home Groups
Co-ordinator will be a key role in the church's
pastoral work.

Effectiveness in this area of church life requires
quite new approaches to leadership, particularly
from the clergy. It will not be easy, but we are
starting to try to tackle it. It is probably a mistake
to 'over-systematise'. More lasting, albeit less
immediate and tangible, results may be achieved
by patient, one-to-one, work, helping individuals
to discover the direction of their pastoral gifts,
to develop them and put them to work in the
areas where they are most appropriate and most

needed. In pursuance of this, Rhys and Gwenda Lewis – who earlier played such a vital role in training carers for the West End – have taken on responsibility for co-ordinating a team of people (whom we have called Lay Pastors) whose task is to keep in touch with members who are, for example, housebound, ill or in some particular need.

3 Unity in the Faith

Relationships with other churches have been a weak point in our past life at St John's. In the 1989 audit this was referred to both by church members and others. It is good to be able to report that early in 1993 St John's joined in signing a covenant with most other Boscombe churches, committing ourselves to work together. But this is only a small beginning. It will require much hard work, and changes in individual attitudes, before it flowers into the kind of effective united evangelism and service which now exists in many towns and cities throughout Britain. Whilst we are excited at the prospect of a united churches' town-wide mission in 1995, early discussions have shown the entrenched attitudes which still remain. John Baker writes:

> We need to ask God to forgive the Church its so frequent petty mindedness, and our putting our own predilections before God's pattern for his Church, and to have mercy upon us ... And we must all make sure we are seeking the good of the Church of Christ in our locality and congregation, and that we are not just seeking to perpetuate what we like at St Blank's. Let us examine ourselves,

and love one another as Christ has loved us,
in the unity of the Spirit.[4]

There is still a good deal of ground to be made up
before Christians in the area begin to appreciate
fully this aspect of their life together.

* * *

St John's faces a number of challenges in the
immediate future:

• The 1989 audit highlighted our lack of
identity with the people of our parish. Although the Open Door meets the needs of
some of those with special problems, the
tentative home visiting early in 1993 showed
this lack of identity still exists. Although this
may be explained by the fact that such a
tiny minority of church members live in the
parish, the problem remains. The idea of a
town wide mission in 1995 originated with St
John's; as other areas of Bournemouth take
it up and plan their own simultaneous local
missions, we must not expect to draw people
from those areas. Our own parish must be the
focus of our own mission activity, which can
only succeed if by then we have *already* built
bridges into the local community at the level
of personal contact.
• The likely evolution of the church into
three or more congregations will necessi-
tate different structures to ensure a balance between cohesion on the one hand and
the necessary degree of independence on the

other. A fresh approach to 'management'
must be developed.

● A church plant will mean losing able,
vibrant Christians from our existing congregations. Members will have to face the
inevitable sense of bereavement.

● Any significant further development of
our work will necessarily involve enlarging
the staff. That will mean increasing our
income to cover one or more additional paid
members. We are already agreed that it is
long overdue to include a woman on the staff.

● With our decision to move into regular
'seeker' presentations we are sailing into
uncharted waters. Giving high priority to the
needs of those completely outside the Church
will involve some costly adjustments.

● Increased attention to pastoring the existing members will require a significant shift in
attitudes amongst leaders and throughout the
congregation.

* * *

Many readers might regard the pace of change
in our life at St John's over the last few years
as phenomenal. By some standards it has been.
Obviously there are those within the church who
have felt unable to keep up. Some have moved to
calmer waters elsewhere; others have clung on
– and they should be given special priority as
pastoral care is developed. But it has not been
change for change's sake. Many of us have a sense
of being propelled, and steered, by God. He has
given us the resources, the people, and the call.

Perhaps it is time to use again a prayer which was recommended to us when we were contemplating the Church of the Open Door:

> Lord, forgive us for calculated efforts to serve you when it is convenient for us to do so, only in those places where it is safe for us to do so, and only with those who make it easy to do so. Lord, forgive us, renew us, send us out as usable instruments that we might take seriously the meaning of the Cross. Amen.

CHAPTER THIRTEEN
WHOSE CHURCH IS IT ANYWAY?

Visiting a nearby church recently, my wife and I were met at the door by a dark-suited man who demanded rather severely 'Are you receiving?'. I was about to reply 'Loud and clear ... Over', when I realised that the question had to do with the number of wafers to be consecrated for Communion. Obviously we were expected to realise that ... just as it was assumed we would know about everything else that happened in what turned out to be the most user-*un*friendly service I have ever attended. As knowledgeable churchgoers from a rather different tradition, we just about coped. But suppose we had been visitors with little or no church background, maybe coming to hear our banns, or seeking God because of personal trouble. We should have been completely excluded and utterly mystified from start to finish ... if, indeed, we had passed the entrance examination at the door! Everybody else seemed to be all right. They all appeared to know what was going on. Obviously they were all regulars. It was *their* church. But was it? How does this inward-looking, proprietorial attitude to the Church come about?

We noted in Chapter Three how the Church of

England came historically to be so closely identified with the nation that the two were virtually
synonymous. That Establishment has survived
down the centuries to the present day; for several hundred years English people have been
allowed, sometimes even encouraged, to think of
themselves as members of the Church without
any particular belief or practice on their part.
(No wonder some clergy's refusal to baptise children without question as to their parents' faith
can cause such shock and genuine distress.) Perhaps this confusion of identity has contributed
to the phenomenon described by David Power
(adviser on evangelism in the Diocese of Exeter)
that 'the Church of England has never really
considered its evangelistic task over the past
450 years'.[1] An ingrained assumption that everybody is really 'in' the Church already is clearly
not the most dynamic motivator for evangelism!
The rapid secularisation of our society, whilst a
cause for deep concern, has at least clarified some
issues; the *need* for evangelism can hardly now be
doubted.

Yet a great many church members still persist
in treating the Church as though it exists solely
for their benefit – in fact as if it belongs to them.
Who does it belong to? Of course there is a legal
answer to that question, and a variety of possible
theological answers. Some readers may (not without a slightly self-satisfied smile) already have
given the 'correct' answer: 'It belongs to God, of
course.' Quite so. But suppose a completely impar-
tial observer were to examine what goes on in your
church and ask for whom, in whose interests, the
whole thing seems to operate. What conclusion

would he come to? For the Vicar . . . the PCC . . .
the choir . . . the churchwardens . . . those who
have been members longest . . . the youth group
. . . the charismatic 'in-group' . . . the uniformed
organisations . . . the Vicar's wife . . . ?

William Temple described the Christian Church
as 'the only institution which exists primarily for
the benefit of non-members'. That word 'primarily' is important – without it the statement would
be incomplete and dangerously misleading. The
over-arching duty and privilege of the Church, as
God's people, is to offer him worship. Then, as the
Body of Christ, all members have a duty to care
for one another and build one another up. But the
primary purpose of its existence is, through word
and deed, to proclaim the gospel of Jesus Christ
to the world. (See Matthew 28:19; 1 Corinthians
10:33.) The Decade of Evangelism aims to recall
the Church to that priority. Its purpose is to bring
others into saving faith in Jesus; and since he
is the Way, the Truth and the Life, the only
name 'under heaven . . . by which we must be
saved' (Acts 4:12) there is no need to apologise
for that.[2]

This primacy of the interests of non-members
has implications across the whole spectrum of a
church's life. It will affect not only the obvious
things like worship style . . . but what other
meetings are held, when and where; what media
and techniques are used in teaching, publicity etc;
what buildings are needed and how they are used;
how funds are raised and allocated. Currently (as
David Cohen, formerly General Director of Scripture Union, points out) 95 per cent of the Church's
resources are spent on 5 per cent of the population.

Once this concept of priority for ministry to
those outside begins to be taken seriously, it
quickly becomes obvious that it is bound to have
far-reaching consequences for everyone inside.
Those who see the Church as *primarily*

   a club for religious people;
   an organiser of fetes and jumble sales;
   a unique repository of language and culture;
   a classical music society;
   a conservator of antiquities;

may well find the implications too horrifying to
contemplate. Such people do exist; we all know
some of them. But what of those millions of members who do have a spiritual understanding of the
Church as Christ's Body on earth? What might it
mean for them? Let me try to answer that, not
in the abstract, but from our own contemporary
experience at St John's. In doing so I must avoid
giving the impression that we started with a policy statement, 'put non-members first' and have
re-orientated our life accordingly. It has not been
at all like that. But as we have sought to follow
God's leading along the course described in this
book, that is in effect what is *starting* to happen.
At the same time we are having to grapple with the
unexpected, and often rather complex, problems
which arise when those outside come inside.

Who are 'the Church'?

But first we have had to discover who we ourselves
are. For centuries the pattern of church life in

Britain has been clergy-dominated. One still hears ordination described as 'going into the Church'! Roy Barker writes

> People will say to a clergyman 'You have a lively church there with lots of willing workers to help you'. The assumption is always that the clergyman is the church. The congregation, particularly the helpers, assist him to be the church.[3]

Of course, the elders of God's people in a particular locality, ordained and lay alike, are to be both respected and supported. (See 1 Thessalonians 5:12–13; 1 Timothy 5:17.) But *they* are not the church. A local church whose life is shaped entirely by the insights, priorities and activities of its ordained minister(s) is a misshapen church. On holiday in the North of England a couple of years ago, my wife and I were much interested by an exercise carried out in one diocese; each parish had done a survey of its life and work, recording the answers to a standard set of questions in an album on display in the church. A great deal of thought and care had obviously gone into many of them. But we particularly remember one beautiful village church. The various facts and organisations were meticulously recorded; the parish priest had described how he saw his role in the parish; but where church members were invited to say 'what my church means to me', the incumbent had written 'Nobody could be persuaded to articulate a response to this question'. That is quite simply one of the saddest things I have ever read.

Every mention of the Church in the New Testament (whether by the Greek words thus translated, or by other terms such as 'God's people' or 'the household of faith') clearly refers to the whole body of believers, not to some ordained elite. It follows that 'the Church's' priorities, ministry and mission are the priorities, ministry and mission of every member. Those local churches which are growing (in both numbers and effectiveness) are often those where the concept of 'every-member ministry' is taken seriously. A rough check at St John's shows that in May 1993 around 190 people were on 'active service' in some way – as teachers, sidespersons, cleaners, housegroup leaders, West End carers and helpers, musicians, drama group, Communion administrants, sound desk operators ... That is over 60 per cent of the adults (aged 15 and over) on the membership roll.[4] I doubt whether comparable national statistics exist; but I am fairly certain this is a phenomenally high proportion.

It is simply not possible for one man, even with a few dedicated helpers, to make any significant impact on the community. (This is now true even in the smallest rural parishes, where the groupings of recent years have diluted the traditionally close relationship between parson and local people.) The local church's response to this is often to concentrate its attention and resources on its own members, interacting with 'outsiders' mainly or only when they come for weddings, baptisms and funerals. As society has grown more secular, the Church has tended to turn in on itself. Realistically, only the mobilisation of 'lay' people on a massive scale can make any significant impact

on the community. Every-member ministry, or
the 'priesthood of all believers', is not just an
evangelical buzzword; nor is it a gimmick to try to
enthuse an apathetic laity. The *laos* is the people
of God – the Church. *The Church* will only fulfil its
primary purpose of proclaiming in word and deed
God's love for the world, if the majority of its *members* do so. This book has introduced the reader
to some folk at St John's who have dedicated
themselves to that purpose; and they represent
many others who have not made these pages by
name. Without their commitment of themselves,
God's work could never have progressed as it has,
however faithful and visionary the leaders.

What is the Church Coming To?

But making evangelism a priority brings with it
a whole new set of 'problems' – though it would
be preferable to regard them as opportunities.
Dealing with the problems – or seizing the opportunities – demands a complete change in thinking
about many aspects of church life which could be
taken more or less for granted all the while a congregation saw itself as a self-perpetuating entity.
Such fundamental changes in thought patterns
are not at all easy.

Worship is the most obvious aspect – and the
most controversial. I am not sure why this should
be so ... unless it is that attending services is
as far as many people's membership goes. The
problem here is summed up forcefully by John
Leach:

We have a God-given responsibility towards
those for whom we have pastoral care in
the congregation ... We have to love them
and strive with the Spirit to present them
mature and spotless to the Father. But we
also have a responsibility to those outside
the Church, to win them to faith in the Lord.
Sometimes those two responsibilities conflict
when those in the Church seem determined,
by their conservatism and intransigence, to
keep the outsiders outside by maintaining the
Church in a state of terminal irrelevance. It
is our job ... to work out those two areas of
responsibility, but if at times we leave behind
those inside, that may be a necessary evil
in order to fulfil our responsibility to those
outside.[5]

Our own tentative plans to introduce 'seeker-
orientated' activities at St John's, if they are to
succeed, will involve quite radical changes in the
way we think, not only about services, but about
priorities in spending time, money and effort.

Gearing churches up to be evangelistic is a big
enough challenge; but it leads on to another, possibly greater, challenge. What if our evangelism
'succeeds'? After all, we should expect it to if we
ourselves are faithful and believe in the saving
power of God in Christ. I suspect the honest truth
is that most of us would not feel too disturbed if
it resulted in just one or two 'outsiders' joining
the church. It need not really affect us very much.
We should probably expect them to come on our
terms anyway – to join in the things we are doing
and to want the things we think will be good for

them. But what if new people started coming in
significant numbers?

It came as something of a surprise to us at St
John's how many of those with whom we have
come into contact through the West End project started coming regularly to services. Already
they represent a significant proportion of the congregation, and some are in every sense 'church
members'. How should we respond to this? Let
me take some practical examples.

* * *

When those 'outside' start coming 'inside', fundamental questions need to be asked about our
worship style – ethos, language, teaching methods,
music, books ... everything needs to be looked at
afresh – through their eyes. This is not some kind
of cheap sell-out of valued traditions in order to
'get more people to come to church'. In the 1960s
and 70s, although the media reaction to 'trendy,
long-haired, guitar-playing clerics' was often ill-
informed and intemperate, there were some real
mistakes and much confused thinking in parts of
the Church. While worship should be enjoyable,
it should never be entertainment. (This is true,
incidentally, whether on a 'popular' or a 'highbrow'
level.) Neither, I believe, is worship itself, *primarily*,
a means of evangelism. But if evangelism on other
fronts (whether through word or deed or both)
brings people with a new faith and no church
background into the worshipping community of the
church, then we must seek to enable them to express
themselves with integrity. We must stop regarding
it as *our* worship, which *they* must join in as best

they can. For those who come seeking God, we must do all in our power to help them. For those who have found him, we must be quite clear that they are now members of his Church just as we are. They may come from a different social class and a very different background from many of us. They may have all kinds of personal problems which are unfamiliar, even distasteful, to us. But they are no longer 'they'; from now on, when we say 'we' it includes them.

That being true, it needs to be made real at every level. When BBC 1's *South Today* carried a short feature about the Open Door in December 1991, several Westenders described what it meant to them – and the word that cropped up over and over again was 'acceptance'. But that does not come easily. Although there is a persistent 'presumption' towards the poor and needy throughout Scripture, and Jesus chose to spend much of his time among the sick, the prostitutes and the social outcasts, somewhere along the line this perspective has been lost. The Church in Britain today is for the most part middle-class and respectable . . . seeking to fill its empty seats, if at all, with more of its own kind. The poor and the social outcasts in our society – the homeless or jobless, those caught in the infamous DSS 'poverty trap', the ex-offender or ex-addict, the disturbed child or mentally-unstable adult – are not thought of by most church members as potential fellow-members.

Let me give two recent instances which demonstrate this. In the first a participant in our caring course dropped out after a 'live' visit to the West End, remarking 'I knew this sort of people existed, but I somehow don't think of them in the context of church'. The second arose in connection with a local ecumenical service being held in St John's. Those involved in leading the service came for a rehearsal; encountering the clientele in the West End, one leader asked if there was some other entrance that could be used in the afternoon so that people attending the service would not have to go in and out through the West End. Nobody was asking them to get involved with these needy folk, but they did not even want to be reminded of their existence . . . not in church . . . on their way into a service. I shuddered when I imagined what the Old Testament prophets – or indeed Jesus himself – would have said about this.

Sometimes an attitude of acceptance will involve facing up to St Paul's principle about limiting our own freedom so as not to risk offending the 'weaker brother'. (See 1 Corinthians 8 and Romans 14.) A relevant example arose over the wine used at Holy Communion services. An increasing number of people are joining in our worship for whom alcohol has been, or still is, a problem. Experts advise that, even for those who appear to have overcome their addiction, the slightest taste (or even the smell) of alcohol can stimulate the craving for more. It is unthinkable that participation in the Holy Communion – the very act which most deeply symbolises their new-found membership amongst God's people – should trigger off a resurgence of the old desires and contribute to their downfall. Sadly, when the PCC discussed this, some members could not seem to see the seriousness of the issue involved and voted according to whether they liked the taste of the non-alcoholic alternative.

* * *

Whilst talking with one of our most dedicated
and experienced carers, I received a poignant challenge about how far I had personally managed to
change my way of thinking about 'us' and 'them'.
At the time we were having severe difficulties
with one young man, whose disturbed behaviour
in the West End was seriously upsetting others
and putting at risk the work we were trying to
do. The carer and her husband had been making
prolonged efforts to help him, offering friendship
and even inviting him into their home for meals.
From the opening of the West End it was made a
rule for carers' own protection that their surname,
telephone number or home address should not be
disclosed to visitors. I asked if she did not think
we had brought the difficulties on ourselves by
breaking the rules in this case. 'But he's become
a personal friend,' she replied, '. . . do you mean
there are some friends from church we're allowed
to invite to lunch and others we're not?' This was
the same carer who said God had enabled her to
'see the person behind the addiction'. Fortunately,
she dealt very graciously with me . . . but I soon
realised that my question, if not actually stupid,
had betrayed a lack of thought and understanding.
When do people stop being *just* Westenders?

That conversation made me realise that although the creation of the Church of the Open
Door was itself a major leap forward in St John's
ministry, much further we have come much further in the four years since. In 1989 the picture
was quite clear. *We* (the church) were called to
open ourselves up to *them* (the needy in the local

community), offering a listening ear, friendship, advice and help. In order to do that effectively and safely, we needed a set of ground rules by which to operate. These were laid down by the Open Door's first manager, Michael Jeffries, with great wisdom and sensitivity. But, basically, what we were then envisaging was a situation where our ministry remained *static*, offered to a constantly-changing clientele. In practice it is to some extent working out the other way around. An unexpected number of people come to stay, some finding faith and some still seeking ... but many joining the church and developing a network of relationships just like any other church member. This requires our ministry to be *dynamic*. It is no longer a clear picture, with church members on one side of a line and Westenders on the other. It is no longer simply us ministering and them being ministered to. The pattern is now so complex that it is sometimes not possible to see it at all. In a way this is a real mark of the 'success' of the Open Door ministry, and as such ought to make us glad. Indeed it does; but at the same time it blurs many of the once firm guidelines.

Risks have to be taken. Some mistakes will be made. Many of the old certainties are gone; in their place a constantly-shifting set of challenges to which there is no standard set of responses, and questions to which there is no 'right' answer. At times this is slightly frightening. The challenges can only go on increasing as those needy, damaged people who have already made their home at St John's are joined by others. All this at the same time as we seek to move into new ways of reaching totally 'un-churched' people.

1981 seems a long time ago now. It was then that
Bishop John Taylor charged us as a congregation
to 'embody the love of God for every man, woman
and child who reside within the boundaries of
this parish'. He went on: 'We must be seen to
be a caring people in the whole neighbourhood
if anybody is to give credit to our claim to have
discovered some special facet and vision of the love
of God for ourselves.'

We have come some way. Doing so has involved
constant change – in our buildings, insights, attitudes and priorities. Searching for one single
factor which both explains and sums up all this
change, past, present and future, I have concluded
it is simply this. We are slowly learning that St
John's does not belong to us to do with as we
wish. It belongs to God; he entrusts it to us for
the benefit of all those he has given us to serve
in his name – those inside, those on the way in,
those outside. Not everybody finds change easy.
Yet, if we are reading the signs of God's call
correctly, there can only be more of it ahead.
One thing is certain: there is no turning back.

Speaking about the wedding in Cana (John 2:
1–11), Bishop John Taylor encouraged us to draw
the living water that is the *contemporary* Christ.
He urged us to look not to our own past, but

to the very source of it all in the Jesus
Christ who is as alive today as he was in
the past. Go back to the ancient springs
of the grace of Christ, of the truth of the
Scripture . . . make the old thing your own,
today – and you will find that it is wonderful
and miraculous.

* * *

*May the God of peace, who through the blood
of the eternal covenant brought back from the
dead our Lord Jesus, that great Shepherd of
the sheep, equip [us] with everything good
for doing his will, and may he work in us
what is pleasing to him, through Jesus Christ,
to whom be glory for ever and ever. Amen.*
(Hebrews 13:20–21)

CHAPTER FOURTEEN
WHAT ABOUT YOU?

We are now almost halfway through the Decade of Evangelism. Its aims are

- praying for the renewing love and power of the Holy Spirit;
- equipping all Christians to live and share the gospel;
- exploring God's activity in different situations and cultures;
- changing whenever necessary the Church's worship, ministry and structures;
- confronting injustice and responding to human need.

This agenda is about a church renewing its inward life, then turning outwards to share God's gifts with the community, in costly service. For many churches that represents a massive change in attitude and priorities.

According to a survey published in May 1993 almost 70 per cent of people in Britain say they believe in God. On the face of it that makes it difficult to understand how our society as a whole can be so secularised. I referred earlier to Archbishop George Carey's assertion that the process of secularisation is complete when 'supernatural faith becomes private and optional'.[1] Could it be that a sizeable proportion of this 70 per cent have precisely this kind of 'private' belief – one which does not significantly affect their own lifestyle or their values as members of society? There is evidence that this is indeed so. A MARC Europe survey of 'nominal Christians' (those who regard themselves as Christians but are not church members or regular attenders) concluded that for such people religion has become –

> *relativised* (with no concept of objective truth);
> *marginalised* (kept out of mainstream society);
> *trivialised* (seen as a hobby or leisure pursuit);
> *sanitised* (not allowed to threaten or challenge).[2]

In the face of that kind of 'belief' the Church's evangelistic task remains urgent. Until people have a personal faith in God which impacts on their lifestyle and moral values, there remains a need to proclaim both his love and his standards for righteous living. But how can the Church effectively call the nation to such values unless it exhibits them in its own life both nationally and locally? How can individual Christians witness effectively to their neighbour about the God who sent his Son to die at Calvary unless their own lives bear the stamp of the cross . . . that is, are marked by self-sacrifice?

There is an indissoluble link between *change* and *sacrifice*. In his Inaugural Speech US President Bill Clinton said, 'The urgent question of our time is whether we can make change our friend, not our enemy.' If he had been addressing the General Synod of the Church of England he could not have hit the nail more squarely on the head! He then went on to speak at some length about the need for *sacrifice* – which one political commentator referred to as 'the dreaded S-word'. How true. This is at the heart of the challenge with which I believe the Holy Spirit is confronting churches and individual Christians today. *The greatest single impediment to change is unwillingness to make sacrifices*.

* * *

Sacrifice is central to the Christian gospel. Jesus made it crystal clear that discipleship is synonymous with self-sacrifice. 'If anyone would come after me, he must deny himself and take up his cross daily and follow me. For whoever wants to save his life will lose it, but whoever loses his life for me will save it' (Luke 9:23–24). Today's culture, by contrast, encourages everyone to believe that they should have what they want – and have it now. To this dangerous idea the last few years have added a selfish individualism which is insidiously anti-Christian. Unhappily, these values have infiltrated the Church so that even there, where we might expect to find the characteristics of true discipleship displayed, we may hear little – and see even less – of the life of self-sacrifice.

As well as our Lord's teaching, we have his own example. He made the ultimate self-sacrifice, without which there would be no Church, no faith,

no salvation and no hope for any of us. His choice
in Gethsemane to accept the call to a sacrificial
death was vindicated by his resurrection. God
the Father demonstrated that his Son's sacrifice
was accepted, and gave him the reward – the
name above all names. This principle, proved by
Jesus, is at the very heart of the Christian faith
and underlies all Christian experience: sacrifice
comes before reward, the cross before the crown,
the suffering before the glory. (See Matthew 19:29;
2 Timothy 2:11–12; Hebrews 12:2; Romans 8:18.)
In Philippians 2:9 the word 'therefore' is crucial:
the glory given to Jesus by his Father was not *in
spite* of his sacrificial death but *because* of it. That
is precisely the point; and Paul develops it in that
chapter not as an abstract theological proposition,
but with the explicit intention (v.5) that we should
adopt the same attitude. He spells out exactly
what this means within the life of the Church
– 'Do nothing out of selfish ambition or vain
conceit, but in humility consider others better
than yourselves. Each of you should look not only
to your own interests, but also to the interests of
others.'

There is nothing novel about this; it is the New
Testament's consistent pattern for living, after
the example of Christ himself. 'Nobody should
seek his own good, but the good of others' (1
Corinthians 10:24). 'We who are strong ought . . .
not to please ourselves. Each of us should please
his neighbour for his good, to build him up. For
even Christ did not please himself . . .' (Romans
15: 1–3). Insofar as we have failed to live this way,
we have been impoverished, both individually and
corporately. But the call to sacrificial living has

special force and logic in the context of the Decade of Evangelism. Giving priority to evangelism will involve massive changes, which cannot be achieved without sacrifices being made.

Since Jesus has proved beyond all possible doubt that the sacrificial principle 'works' and issues in immeasurable blessing, what is it that makes Christians hold back from following it wholeheartedly? Is it that we all have 'un-redeemed' enclaves in our lives which as yet remain closed to God? What are the points in your life, or that of your church, where self-centredness still dominates thoughts and actions? Is it,

● fighting for personal preferences in such things as music, language and worship patterns?
● striving to influence plans and activities according to personal views, instead of learning to seek God's will together?
● placing limits on commitment in prayer, time and giving?
● concentrating attention and energy on what is got out of *services* to the exclusion of what is put into *service*?
● allocating a minimal proportion of time and resources to efforts to reach those outside the Church with the gospel?

These things, and others like them, must be brought to God in personal and corporate repentance before we can look for the renewing power of the Holy Spirit to touch our lives and turn us outwards to others rather than inwards on ourselves.

Ultimately, accepting self-sacrifice as the basis

for living is not only necessary in order to allow the Church to become more outward-looking, it is itself the very quality which, more than any other, will recommend the gospel to the world. A community visibly living for others – especially at the level of the local church – will be so startlingly *different* that the world cannot help but sit up and take notice. This is the very mark of the presence of Christ's kingdom on earth. 'All life in the kingdom will essentially be life for others; life outside . . . is always predictably every man for himself.'[3]

It has been well said that 'the church that lives to itself will die by itself'. Many churches today face a situation where the only thing obviously growing is the cost of maintaining the status quo. Realistically, without radical changes in outlook and priorities, such churches cannot survive for much longer. This is the conclusion of Bishop Michael Marshall, from his wide experience as pastor, theologian and academic. He writes: 'alongside many continuing practices of Anglicanism, there simply must be some radical ingredients of change if Anglicanism, humanly speaking, is to survive into the next century.'[4]

But the case for change does not depend primarily on the threat of annihilation. After all, to change merely in order to survive may still be, basically, self-centred. It rests on our obedience to Christ's call to give up our own lives for his sake and the gospel's.

With the Decade of Evangelism almost half run, how far has the church to which you belong progressed with its aims? Can you point to ways in which you are more effectively being 'salt' and

'light' in the community in which you are set?
Was there a vision which has faded – because of
timidity or unwillingness to face up to the cost of
fulfilling it? Or are you precisely where you were
five years ago, satisfied simply to have weathered
the storms of change all around you?

* * *

Those of us privileged to be serving God at St
John's, Boscombe at this exciting period in its
history would be the first to admit that we have
got many things wrong and missed many opportunities. So in ending on a note of challenge I should
not want it to be thought for one moment that I
do so from some supposed position of superiority.
If that impression has emerged anywhere in the
course of this book, I seek now to correct it. We
stand as much in need of repentance for past
and present failures as anyone could. Moreover,
the possibilities now facing us for further change
and growth, while they are exciting, contain many
potential pitfalls and very real dangers of 'doing
our own thing' and missing God's will.

'Christ does not ask for our support; he demands
our obedience.'[5] It has been our experience that,
when we have obeyed the vision God has given us,
he has provided our needs and prospered his work
among us. And it is especially in those areas where
we have allowed God to change our attitudes and
priorities, putting to death our own ideas and
aspirations if necessary, that we have seen his
work grow, to the blessing of those in both church
and community.

We hope this story of God at work today in and

through unexceptional people in an 'ordinary'
church will have left you feeling stirred (if not
shaken!). As I wrote at the end of the Introduction,
'If it can happen to us, it can certainly happen to
you'. We could all do no better than make St Paul's
words in 2 Corinthians 4:5 both the test and the
inspiration for all our ministry:

Jesus Christ as Lord, ourselves as . . .
   servants.

APPENDIX

Address given by the Bishop of Winchester, Rt.
Rev John Taylor at the Institution of Rev Godfrey
Taylor to St John's, Boscombe, 16 January 1981

It is always for me a great joy, and also at the
same time a heavy responsibility, to come to the
moment of instituting into a new task and care of
souls someone whom I have known and learned
to love; because it is a great burden that any
man undertakes in these days, to give spiritual
leadership, and to take upon himself the special
responsibility of intercession and prayer for all the
people of a parish.

I want first to emphasise that phrase 'all the
people of a parish'. Very briefly, you will see
that the Service, which is really self-explanatory,
falls into three parts. There is what you might
call the Bishop's part; then there is the part of
local groups; and then there is the part of the
Archdeacon. The Bishop's part is to institute into
the parish the man who has been chosen and
presented to him by the Trustees, the Patrons.
In that part there is almost no mention of a
church or of a congregation. The essential act is
making Godfrey responsible to embody the love

of God for every man, woman and child, who reside within the boundaries of this parish. It is concerned with community. He undertakes – but, of course, not alone – *you* undertake to live for this community in the name of Christ. A parish isn't just a church boundary; it's a civic boundary. It has been always, and always will be; and that is the special glory and the special task of the Church of England as the national Church. It means undertaking responsibility for everyone, even if that responsibility simply consists of making sure that another church and their Minister are taking charge of that person; but if there is no church responsible, then it is *our* church that must be. I have said it's a responsibility for embodying the love of God for every person, in the whole neighbourhood – no one left out.

Now there are a great many people who are embodying the love of God; some of them will stand forward as representatives of different kinds of service in the community – the social workers, the police, those who are in the schools teaching, the District Nurse ... one could go on all the evening enumerating people who, if only they saw it this way, might understand that they, in their own way, are embodying God's love for this community, God's hope and desire for the whole community, that it might begin to reflect the rule of his kingdom. And so Godfrey shares that ministry with a great many other people. He wants their help, and he would like them to receive his help. But within that general expression of love and care, which is God's, there is the *special* responsibility of the Christian folk who, by the grace of God, have learned to understand

that God's love is expressly shown forth in the
experience we have of Jesus Christ. There the
love is focussed; there the love is made effective
through the dying and rising of our Lord, bringing
the grace that bridges the gap between man and
God, reconciling and making us one again, as we
were always meant to be. And so we Christian
people have that special, additional responsibility
of trying to live in such a way that we share our
faith with this whole community. But you cannot
separate the sharing of the faith that we have
from the embodiment of the love which is God's.
We must be seen to be a *caring* people in the whole
neighbourhood if anybody is to give credit to our
claim to have discovered some special facet and
vision of the love of God for ourselves.

And so Godfrey takes on those two tasks, which
are one task; and he looks to you, the Christian congregation, to share with him both the
embodiment of love and the proclamation of our
experience of Christ. And that is for the whole
neighbourhood.

And then there is the welcome, when first of all
representatives of other services in the neighbourhood welcome him as a co-partner, and he receives
their welcome. Then there will be others representing more specifically this congregation and its
leadership. Then there will be the other congregations of the Deanery represented, welcoming him
into the Anglican fellowship of this whole place.
And then there will be also the representatives
of other denominations who come to see in him a
fellow-worker, and he receives their welcome and
offers them his partnership. So we have that whole
picture of people knit together in a single task.

And then at that point – and not till then – we, as it were, concentrate down more closely upon this building and those who are normally here for the purpose of worship and fellowship. At that moment the Archdeacon, who has received my mandate, comes forward, and he undertakes the business of saying (as it were) to Godfrey, 'Now, you've seen this enormous task that you have undertaken with others; would you by any chance find a church come in useful? And a church hall might come in handy, and you probably need a vicarage ... well, all right, I hand those material means, those instruments and tools for the job, into your hands so that you may take up this task more effectively.' Now that puts things in the right order of priority. We are not a sect, and you haven't just got a new manager for a religious club. You are something ever so much greater than that; you are God's mission to that whole area of Bournemouth that is named St John's. With your new Vicar you dedicate yourselves this evening to be aware of that outward-looking task, a specific neighbourhood that is made *your* responsibility. May God give you grace in the years that lie ahead to be faithful in that task, and to see fruit borne for the glory of God.

One last word, and it arises from the Gospel which will probably be the first Gospel Godfrey will read when he celebrates in this church. Next Sunday, Second after Epiphany, tells the story of Cana of Galilee, the turning of water into wine. I think John tells that story, as everything else in his Gospel, with a particular message in mind. To say that doesn't mean that the story didn't happen; but out of the hundreds of stories that

were available, John tells us at the end of his
Gospel that 'these things are written that you
may believe – and I could have filled volumes
with other incidents, but I have chosen these
because they say something'. Well, here comes
the story of water and wine, and immediately we
are reminded that the other Gospels tell us that at
that early stage in his ministry Jesus was talking
a lot about wine – new wine, and how impossible
it is to put it into old bottles . . . and I am certain
that that teaching is linked with this story. So the
story is a kind of acted parable. It is actually about
the new teaching.

What happened? They ran out of wine, and
immediately Jesus saw the possible significance.
So he says to the servants in secret first of all, 'Fill
the stone water-pots up to the brim. Go to the well,
draw water, fill up the water pots.' Those water
pots (St John tells us) were for the purification
of the Jews; they represented the *old* regime,
the law that God had laid down, the religious
structure that had been built up, which consisted
so much of purifications in order that men might
be presented to God. Those huge stone water jars
were representative of the old way, the Law. 'I
didn't come to destroy the Law', Jesus said, '*but
to fulfil it*: so fill them up to the brim with the
water that they are meant to contain.' And that
was done. And then (St John says) Jesus turned
to the servants and said 'Draw out now.' And that
word 'draw out' is only used to draw water from
a well. It's used again in Chapter Four, when he is
talking to the woman of Samaria about drawing
water from the well. It can't mean 'decant from
those stone jars'; and if we think that that's what

happened we have misunderstood the story, and we have certainly misunderstood the point of the story. Jesus says 'All right ... the stone jars are filled up: they have done their work, the days of the old law are fulfilled. Now, go back to the well, and draw out *now* for a new day. Go back to the same source, but draw out for your *contemporary* purposes.'

And this, I think, is a message for our congregation. You have a magnificent past, to which you can look back with thankfulness. I have recently been reading the biography of Max Warren, my great predecessor in the CMS. There it speaks of his days as a curate here at St John's, and one could enumerate so many others who have known the resources of God for their day. But it is no good Godfrey going back to Max Warren's day; it's no good Godfrey trying to draw for his task from that tradition of your past. That isn't where he has to go, not to the stone water-jars; but back to the source from which all those other people drew, the only source there is, the Living Water that is the *contemporary* Christ. And so let him and yourselves not look to your own past, but look to the very source of it all in the Jesus Christ who is as alive today as he was in the past. Go to the source. Draw out NOW, and your water will turn into wine; your water will meet the moment's need of this particular marriage feast and the trouble that people have got into. That's the message of this story. Draw out NOW! Go back to the ancient springs of the grace of Christ, of the truth of the Scripture. Don't rely on a past tradition, but make the old thing *your own*, today, and you will find that it is wonderful and miraculous.

NOTES

Chapter 2

1. For more background to this whole area see Walter L. Arnstein, *Protestant v. Catholic in Mid-Victorian England* (Columbia & London, University of Missouri Press, 1982).
2. Eddie Gibbs, *I believe in Church Growth* (London, Hodder & Stoughton, 1981) pp 432/3.

Chapter 3

1. Michael Ramsey, *The Anglican Spirit* (Boston USA, Cowley Publications, 1991) pp 59ff. In this connection he cites particularly the doctrines of Justification by Faith and the Real Presence.
2. David Watson, *I Believe in the Church* (London, Hodder & Stoughton, 1978) p 82.
3. David Watson, ibid. pp 80/81.
4. Michael Marshall, *The Anglican Church Today and Tomorrow* (London & Oxford, Mowbray, 1984) p 126.
5. These two views are in essence the respective ecclesiology of the Calvinist and Arminian tendencies which have divided Christian thought for centuries. The former emphasises the essentially *exclusive* nature of God's grace in electing a people (the Remnant) to be faithful to him, called out from, and therefore not identical with any part of, the visible Church. Only God knows those who are his; but this 'true' Church is presented throughout Scripture as a small minority. The opposite viewpoint emphasises the essentially *inclusive* nature of God's grace, freely available to all. Because God

wants 'everyone to come to repentance' (2 Peter 3:9), his Church has a perpetual responsibility for mission in word and deed to the world of which it is a part. In its outworking, Calvinism tends to produce a preoccupation with the salvation of the individual soul, and a 'closed' affinity with others of similar outlook. Arminianism tends to gloss over God's judgment of individuals, thus blunting the edge of the Christian gospel. In the Church of England, for example, it gives rise to the 'charitable assumption' that all in fellowship with the visible Church are in good standing with God, leading to such practices as indiscriminate infant baptism. Both sets of ideas are essentially Scriptural: but following either to its extreme, at the expense of the other, leads to heresy. It is worth noticing that both the elect 144,000 (Revelation 14:1–5) and the multitude that no one can count (Revelation 7:9–17) make their appearance in the book of Revelation.

Chapter 4
1. John Finney, *Finding Faith Today: How does it happen?* (Swindon, The Bible Society, 1992).

Chapter 5
1. *Faith in the City: The Report of the Archbishop of Canterbury's Commission on Urban Priority Areas* (London, Church House Publishing, 1985) paragraphs 5.2–5.9, pp 82–84.
2. Ibid. paragraphs 5.37–5.40, pp 91/92, and Appendix A, pp 367–372.
3. All such information was from the 1981 census. This meant it was eight years out of date at the time of the Parish Audit. It has not been possible to provide updates here because at the time of going to press the 1991 census statistics are not yet available broken down into such localised format.
4. George Carey, *The Great God Robbery* (London, Fount Paperbacks, 1989) p 14.
5. All or some of the following publications may be found useful:
    An Audit for the Local Church (London, Church House Publishing, 1985).

John Finney, *The Well Church Book – A practical guide to mission audit* (London/Warwick, Scripture Union/Church Pastoral Aid Society, 1991).

John Cole, *How To Be A Local Church* (Bury St Edmunds, Kevin Mayhew, 1990).

Parish Project – A Resource Book for Parishes to Review their Mission (London, HarperCollins, 1992).

Action in Mission 1 – Evaluation (Baptist Department of Mission, 1992).

Sharing in God's Mission – a programme for the living church (Peterborough, Methodist Publishing House).

Chapter 6

1. Brian Wren, 'There's a spirit in the air' – see for example at No. 246 in *Hymns for Today's Church* (London, Hodder & Stoughton, 1982).

Chapter 8

1. Robert Warren, *On the Anvil* (Crowborough, Highland Books, 1990) p 74.

2. Laurie Green, *Power to the Powerless – Theology Brought to Life* (Basingstoke, Marshall Pickering, 1987) p 71. This is one of a number of striking parallels between our own experiences in the Church of the Open Door and those of the inner city parish of St Chad's in Birmingham, who opened an advice centre for local people living in the shadow of 'Spaghetti Junction'. The story of this endeavour, and what was learnt from it, is movingly told in this remarkable book.

3. Ibid. p 73.

Chapter 9

1. Basil Hume, *Towards a Civilisation of Love – Being Church in Today's World* (London, Hodder & Stoughton, 1988) p 167.

2. Ibid. See especially Chapter 12 for an extremely clear and powerful exposition of this whole subject.

3. This danger has perhaps been most apparent in recent years in the 'liberation theology' developed in parts

of the Third World. This not only emanated from the
Church's experience under unjust or oppressive regimes,
but went on to be the dominant factor determining both
its theology and its role. Without doubt this was a
very necessary emphasis; but its apotheosis ('Jesus
the Revolutionary') is a one-sided gospel, which can be
positively dangerous when applied to situations quite
different from that out of which it was born.

4. Quoted by Michael Ramsey in *The Anglican Spirit*
(Boston USA, Cowley Publications, 1991) pp 96/97.

5. Clive Calver: article 'Melding Evangelicals into an
effective force in the nation' in the *Church Times*, 7
February 1992.

6. 'We dare not retreat into a state of spiritualised individualism. The New Testament is full of texts which
urge us to respond to the needs of our neighbours.
Our Lord left us stories like Dives and Lazarus, the
Good Samaritan ... and the account of Judgement
Day. St John questioned: 'If a man who was rich
enough in this world's goods saw that one of his
brothers was in need, but closed his heart to him,
how could the love of God be living in him?' ...
The Church, however, has come to realise over the
centuries that ... it is not sufficient simply to react
to emergencies but to seek where possible to identify
the root cause of the problem, to tackle it and to try
to ensure it does not recur ... Since so many social
issues are matters of morality, at the very least one
must continue to uphold the Church's role as the
conscience of international and national society.' Basil
Hume, *Towards a Civilisation of Love – Being Church
in Today's World* (London, Hodder & Stoughton, 1988),
pp 165–167.

7. Laurie Green, op. cit. In relation to institutionalised
oppression see especially chapters 6 and 7. (See also
notes 2 and 3 to Chapter 8 above.)

8. Michael Marshall, *The Anglican Church Today and
Tomorrow* (London & Oxford, Mowbray, 1984) p 9.

9. The decisions I instance are those which will need
to be worked out at local level. The renewal of the
whole Church for service would imply a need for
potentially radical decisions about structures, worship,

establishment and where power lies in the institutional
Church.

Chapter 10

1. There is a three-tier treatment system for addictive
    and psychological disorders. Primary Treatment Centres
    provide intensive treatment (including detoxification
    where necessary). Patients are then sent to Secondary
    Treatment Centres known as 'half-way houses' for con-
    solidation, further counselling and group work. When
    they are thought to be ready (a minimum of three
    months) they are moved on to Tertiary Treatment
    Centres, or 'dry houses'. In St John's geographically-tiny
    parish there are no less than six Secondary and Tertiary
    centres, five of them within a quarter of a mile. This
    exceptional concentration of people with special needs
    (many of them issuing in relationship or behavioural
    difficulties) gives rise to severe problems for GPs and
    other welfare agencies. It also produces a critical need
    for the church's ministry of listening, acceptance and
    friendship.
2. Charles Swindoll, *The Grace Awakening* (Dallas, Texas,
    Word Incorporated, 1990 and Milton Keynes, Word (UK)
    Ltd, 1990) p 229.
3. Ibid. p. 303.
4. Donald Coggan, *Cuthbert Bardsley, Bishop, Evangelist,
    Pastor* (London, Collins, 1989) pp 207/8.
5. Graham Kendrick's song 'The Servant King' may be
    found in most newer song and hymn books. See, for
    example, *Songs of Fellowship* (Eastbourne, Kingsway,
    1992).
6. Laurie Green, p 80. Op cit. (See also notes 2 and 3 to
    Chapter 8 above.)

Chapter 11

1. This whole subject is difficult and cannot be treated in
    a book of this nature. Readers who may be tempted to
    regard this suggestion as fanciful are recommended to
    read and reflect on Ephesians 6:11–12 and 1 Peter 5:8.
    See also especially 2 Corinthians 2:10–11: St Paul clearly

regarded broken or unforgiving relationships within the
Church as typical of 'Satan's schemes'.

Chapter 12

1. P. Simmonds, *Reaching the Unchurched: Some Lessons
    from Willow Creek*, Grove Booklet on Evangelism 19
    (Bramcote, Grove Books, 1992).
2. Robert Warren, *In the Crucible* (Crowborough, Highland
    Books, 1989) see especially Chapter 12.
3. See note 1 to Chapter 11. 1 Thessalonians 2:18 ('Satan
    stopped us') appears to give reason to believe that there
    are occasions when those seeking to carry out some par-
    ticular work for God are prevented by Satan from doing
    so. Our own experience here is yet another parallel with
    the story of the opening of a community advice centre at
    St Chad's, Birmingham told in *Power to the Powerless*
    (see note 2 to Chapter 8), where the group 'experienced
    the most extraordinary run of illness and grief' including
    three deaths and a stroke (pp 134, 135). They noted,
    positively, that their own deep sense of powerlessness
    in the face of these tragedies stimulated a tenderness
    which enhanced their ministry to the powerless people
    around them. To maintain a balance it is vital to hold
    on to the truth that God in his grace can always bring
    blessing for his people out of whatever Satan may inflict
    on them.
4. John P Baker (ed), *Christ's Living Body*, (London &
    Eastbourne, Coverdale House, 1973). pp 23/24.

Chapter 13

1. Quoted in the article 'Success of "Decade"' confounding
    critics, says Bishop' in the *Church of England News-
    paper*, 1 May 1992.
2. Even as I was writing this sentence a light aeroplane
    flew past towing a banner DIANETICS THE OWNERS
    (sic) MANUAL FOR THE HUMAN MIND. If Christians
    do not reach people with the unique, life-giving news
    of God's gift of forgiveness and freedom in Christ,
    there are plenty of other people peddling counterfeit
    alternatives.
3. L Roy Barker's essay 'Patterns of Congregational Life'

in *Christ's Living Body* edited by John P Baker (London and Eastbourne, Coverdale House, 1973) p 62.

4. Our own working list of members' names and addresses, as distinct from the Electoral Roll.

5. John Leach, *Liturgy and Liberty* (Tunbridge. Wells, MARC, 1989) p 253.

Chapter 14

1. George Carey, *The Great God Robbery* (London, Fount Paperbacks, 1989) p 14.

2. Survey results published in High Summer 1992 edition of *LandMARC – Information to Steer By* (London, MARC Europe).

3. Michael Marshall, *The Anglican Church Today and Tomorrow* (London & Oxford, Mowbray, 1984) p 156.

4. Ibid. p 153.

5. Cuthbert Bardsley, quoted by Donald Coggan in *Cuthbert Bardsley, Bishop, Evangelist, Pastor* (London, Collins, 1989) p 88.